I would like to personally endorse this written work of art authored by Bishop Ángel L. Núñez, who embodies and models the multicultural movement seen throughout Baltimore and the Mid-Atlantic Region and beyond. He continues to build bridges that connect the faith base as a resource to the needs and demands of today's communities. This book will challenge you to step out of your comfort zone and become what you have been called to be.

—Bishop Marcus A Johnson, Sr.
New Harvest Ministries, Inc., Senior Pastor / Founder
Apostolic Ministerial Alliance, Vice-President
African American Leadership Forum for Public Safety,
Co-Chair

I have known Bishop Ángel Núñez for many years. He is a gifted communicator with a heart for building bridges within the church and a passion for influencing the secular culture of our day.

Rev. Núñez and the Multicultural Prayer Movement have been used of God to help calm Baltimore City's troubled waters—a nearly impossible task. Although there is still much work to be done, they have developed a practical prototype that will help our nation move forward.

Bishop Núñez's secret sauce has been faith in God, trust in others, and tireless service. He is a friend and confidant recognized by governors, mayors, city council members, clergy, police officers, business owners, and urban youth of all races.

The Multicultural Prayer Movement, Bishop Núñez, and other courageous leaders patrolled the troubled streets of "violence-torn" Baltimore in the spring of 2015, armed only with crosses and the Word of God. The strategies Baltimore clergy have used during the last few years have set a standard for the church nation-wide. The question this book presents and answers is this: "How do you transform tense, troubled communities into productive, peaceful places?" The pattern, principles, process, and product of a new kind of prayer movement are laid out in the pages of this book. Faith plus works are at the center of this movement. I hope you are ready for a bloodless, spiritual revolution. The nation needs one!

—Bishop Harry R. Jackson, Jr.
Hope Christian Church and
The Reconciled Church Initiative

THE MULTICULTURAL PRAYER ARMY

THE MULTICULTURAL PRAYER ARMY

Bishop Dr. Ángel L. Núñez

Dare to Dream!
Bishop

CREATION HOUSE

THE MULTICULTURAL PRAYER ARMY by Ángel L. Núñez
Published by Creation House
A Charisma Media Company
600 Rinehart Road
Lake Mary, Florida 32746
www.charismamedia.com

This book or parts thereof may not be reproduced in any form, stored in a retrieval system, or transmitted in any form by any means—electronic, mechanical, photocopy, recording, or otherwise—without prior written permission of the publisher, except as provided by United States of America copyright law.

Unless otherwise noted, all Scripture quotations are from the New King James Version of the Bible. Copyright © 1979, 1980, 1982 by Thomas Nelson, Inc., publishers. Used by permission.

Scripture quotations marked NLT are from the Holy Bible, New Living Translation, copyright © 1996, 2004, 2007. Used by permission of Tyndale House Publishers, Inc., Wheaton, IL 60189. All rights reserved.

Scripture quotations marked AMP are from the Amplified Bible. Old Testament copyright © 1965, 1987 by the Zondervan Corporation. The Amplified New Testament copyright © 1954, 1958, 1987 by the Lockman Foundation. Used by permission.

Design Director: Justin Evans
Cover design by Rachel Lopez

Copyright © 2016 by Ángel L. Núñez
All rights reserved.

Visit the author's website: www.mc-pm.net

Library of Congress Cataloging-in-Publication Data: 2016933816
International Standard Book Number: 978-1-62998-530-5
E-book International Standard Book Number: 978-1-62998-531-2

While the author has made every effort to provide accurate telephone numbers and Internet addresses at the time of publication, neither the publisher nor the author assumes any responsibility for errors or for changes that occur after publication.

First edition

16 17 18 19 20 — 9 8 7 6 5 4 3 2 1
Printed in Canada

As we embark on the journey of life and ministry, there are people God places in our lives to help us reach our destination. I would like to take a moment to thank some of them for imparting, not only to this book, but also to my life.

Therefore, I give thanks and dedicate this book to:

Bishop John Stout, for being a true covenant brother and a prophetic voice in my life.

Bishop Marcus Johnson, for having the courage to stand with me in the good, the bad, and the ugly.

Bishop Emilio Martinez, for being my mentor and model of not only what a minister, but also of what a father and a friend, should be. Note: Bishop Emilio Martinez went to be with the Lord on January 6, 2014; he is sorely missed.

Bishop Don Meares, for helping to shape and form my prophetic insight from a distance, leaving an eternal deposit in my inner being.

Pastor Deborah Núñez (my wife), for standing with me as a prophetess, a pillar of strength, and a fountain of encouragement throughout my entire journey.

The Bilingual Christian Church, for their continued commitment to the vision that God has given me and to the Multicultural Prayer Movement; love you all.

My Heavenly Father, for taking me out of the streets of New York City, saving me, and setting me in places that I would have never imagined.

TABLE OF CONTENTS

Introduction xiii
Chapter One: Where Is the Unity? 1
Chapter Two: Unity Provokes the Supernatural........ 11
Chapter Three: Anointing Oil 19
Chapter Four: An Open Heaven 27
Chapter Five: The Battle that Is before Us..............35
Chapter Six: Speaking Truth to Power................41
Chapter Seven: Change of Mind 53
Chapter Eight: Under Siege 61
Chapter Nine: Prayer Altars.........................71
Chapter Ten: The Building of a
    Multicultural Prayer Army.....................79
Chapter Eleven: This Little Light of Mine.............85
Chapter Twelve: Preparing for
    What Has Been Prepared for Us 95
About the Author................................ 101
Contact the Author 103

INTRODUCTION

TWENTY-SEVEN YEARS AGO, we (my wife Deborah and I) arrived in Baltimore with orders from God to raise an army of warriors for the kingdom of heaven. We had no understanding of what that meant. Our understanding of pastoring was gained from the perspective of shepherding sheep and not of building a spiritual military force.

During the first few years of our ministry here in Baltimore, we came to perceive that God wanted more than just a Hispanic army; He wanted a multicultural, multiethnic army that modeled kingdom unity by answering the prayer that Jesus made in John 17. With that leading, we became a bilingual ministry, and at present, the congregation has the seed of 23 nations that worship together under one roof at the same time. This is our testimony, our presentation to show the world that it is possible for all of God's people to come together as one force.

We have always been keenly aware of the fact that we are not the army of God, but a division within that prayer army. We understand that we need to find like-minded men and women of God with whom we would enter into covenant and cause a transformation to occur, not only in our city, but across North America and even beyond.

As the years went by, the vision started to become clearer and clearer, but the people could not fully grasp or understand it because I could not cast the vision with clarity since I myself was still trying to take hold, understand, and steward the task that God had given me.

Five years ago, as I was sitting in a leadership conference in West Virginia, the Lord spoke to me through prophets who were in the house that I was to return to Baltimore and blow the trumpet for the army of God to gather in prayer. However, I was not to promote it or make it into an event. Rather, those who were of the same spirit would hear the sound of the trumpet in their inner being and response to the call of unity. Of course, this did not make any sense to me, but I obeyed the Lord and blew the trumpet.

The first man of God to appear was Bishop Marques Johnson (Pastor Johnson at that time). He is an African-American pastor that God connected me to through a South African bishop of Indian descent who came to Baltimore to minister at Pastor Johnson's church. He had heard of me and insisted that Pastor Johnson meet me.

Our relationship exploded as we shared, compared backgrounds, and realized that we had been doing the same thing in the same area of the city, and yet never crossed over that invisible divider to connect with each other or even to consider worshiping together. We vowed that would never happen again, and both churches started looking for ways to do ministry and acts of kindness together. We became *one* church in two locations. As we continued our journey in unity, we realized that we were not alone, that God had given this vision to others and we needed to find and unite with them.

About this time, Bishop Samuel Rodriguez, president of the NHCLC, and I (senior vice-president of the same organization at that time) started speaking about tearing down the so-called black-brown divide that was being promoted around the nation by groups that wanted to keep Blacks and Hispanics divided. We held a summit in Dallas, TX, which birthed an African-American / Hispanic pastors' summit in Baltimore, MD, that drew about 1,700 pastors and leaders from both groups. Yet, I still longed to connect at a deep level with Anglo pastors from around the region since my passion has always been to bring true unity to the body of Christ.

One day I received a visit from two Anglo pastors; one was a close friend of mine, and the other I previously met. They informed me about a group of pastors called "Partners for Transformation," who had been praying together for transformational revival across this area. Their spirit of humility impressed me, and I invited them to come and share with me. Soon about 20 or more pastors came to meet with me, answered my questions, and invited us to partner with them. We accepted, and for the first time, I caught a glimpse of God's multiethnic, multicultural army taking form. This was a movement that was starting to take form from the bottom up and not from the top down.

During these last five years, we have been praying and meeting together, and I have prayerfully waited, asking God to show us how He wants His vision advanced. The challenge has been getting everyone, including new pastors that join the teams, to understand the importance of raising an army of God and to put aside their own agendas for something greater than any of us. Before, we had different groups praying; Whites, Hispanics, and Blacks were all praying, yet rarely coming together as one. Our challenge was to bring them together.

In the meantime, I continued to see, hear, and read

about the destruction of America from within. Economics, violence, and moral failure combined with a divided church have placed this nation on a course that will soon destroy it. Our nation needs to again hear the voice of God through a united church that speaks truth to power in love. I believe that we have been called to be the moral conscience of this country. This can only been done through a church that speaks with one voice the message of restoration in love.

After my consecration as bishop, the Lord called me to a time of prayer and fasting. During this time, it was made clear in my spirit that the time had come to activate the prayer army with the specific task of releasing the oil of unity among God's people. As I prayed, I could hear in my heart, over and over again, the Spirit of the Lord say, "Unity provokes the supernatural, and when the supernatural is provoked, it will invade the natural."

The purpose of this book is to provoke you to play your note in this symphony of music and thus create a sound of heaven that will cause the supernatural to invade our natural with a demonstration of His glory that will touch His creation, once again—that those who are in darkness can see the hope of glory and live again.

This requires a life that is set apart, a life that is covered by the love of God and that has no problem doing anything to serve. I know that time is running out; therefore, I must resign from all distractions and do what I have been called to do before He calls me home. Consider joining the Multicultural Prayer Movement and bring hope to a dying nation in Jesus's name.

At present, you can join the movement by going to www.mc-pm.net. This way we are able to keep you informed of what we are doing—nothing more, nothing less.

Every individual plays his own note, but when he unites with another, together they create a harmony, a sound that reaches the heavens.

Chapter One
WHERE IS THE UNITY?

THE WORD *UNITY* means a lot of things to a lot of people. It seems that everyone has their own opinion of what unity means and, of course, how it should be implemented. I think the word *unity* has been so misused and abused by so many people that today few want to associate themselves with the term; our enemy has successfully taken unity and used it to keep us apart.

For the sake of this book, I want to clarify that to me unity does not mean you now have to close down your church and unite with another congregation that has a similar vision. Two can come together for a common cause and still not have unity. This is not about shutting down your ministry and joining mine as many would think; this is about partnership, and this is about attracting the presence of God for kingdom purposes.

For me, it is not the word *unity* that's so important but rather what sound unity *creates*. Allow me to explain. Every individual (ministry) plays his own note, but when he unites with another player, *together* they create a harmony that reaches the souls of people and the heavens above. Therefore, there is always diversity in unity because you have to enter into a partnership with someone who is not like you to create harmony. This requires you to be willing to pay a cost. That cost is that you will not be the only player in this sound that serenades both heaven and

Earth. The only possible way for us to do this is to enter and dwell in His glory or presence (I will speak more about this later in the chapter).

In America, we have such an independent spirit embedded in our culture that it transfers into every area of our lives. This mindset is displayed in our ministries, our lives, and in everything we have and do. We have to be the best, the largest, and the most gifted.

When we speak of teamwork, we only speak of it in the context of our local church and not outside of it. We may have twenty keyboard players in our congregation, yet we refuse to share one of them to help a new ministry that is starting up down the street from us. Why? Because we have forgotten that the success of the mission requires us to be one; Father let them be one…so that the world would believe.

Our reality is this: the ground is shaking, the winds are blowing, and the waters are coming out of the sea. Nature is screaming: "The end is coming! The end is coming!" Yet no one is listening. We face an economic disaster that will shake the very core of the way we live. People have lost their homes, jobs, and retirements, yet this is just the beginning of what is to come. Add to that the spirit of immorality, violence, and witchcraft that is invading every fiber of our society, and we can conclude that we are in deep trouble.

What bothers me the most is that we have a divided church that is more interested in entertaining people than in travailing prayer, extravagant worship, or signs and wonders. We are producing preachers who live a double life, are more interested in fame and fortune, and seek to build their own kingdom instead of the kingdom of God. How can we protest and point out the sins of politicians and secular leaders in our country when we ourselves are stained by the sin that besets us?

We talk about unity, but just about every time I hear someone recite John 17:22, I hear them focus on the need for unity within the body of Christ. Even though that is true and necessary, I have come to understand that before we can actually have unity, we need to get in, live in, and walk in the glory of God.

In His final prayer for His disciples, Jesus said, "I have given to them the glory and honor You have given Me, that they may be one [even] as We are one" (John 17:22, AMP).

So what is the glory of God? We know that the Hebrew word for glory is *kabowd,* which means, in a good sense, the weight of something. Glory also speaks of splendor, greatness, abundance, honor, and goodness, among other things.

But for the purposes of our conversation, I would like to use this phrase: nothing is withheld. Therefore, if I am to receive everything He has for me, I will need to be transformed. I must begin a lifelong journey of being transformed into His image so I can receive and walk in His glory.

Transformation is not a one-time thing. It must continue to happen in our lives as we continue to walk in His ways. Spiritual stagnation begins when the presence and power of God cease to operate in our lives. When this happens, everything becomes a routine, and we fall away.

But when we begin to change into His image, our faith begins to increase, our mind begins to change, and we begin to think and act as He would. Our insecurities and prejudices are removed as agape love takes center stage in our lives. It is then that we are capable of going from glory to glory, from victory to victory, and from grace to grace because we are being transformed into the mature image of God.

This change affects the way we hear the Word of God; it influences our approach; it provokes us to seek His wisdom as consistent and new revelations invade our very hearts. No longer are we interested in our own agendas, but in doing the will of the Father. We become kingdom minded, and our passion is to walk and live in His presence.

Religious people obey the Word of God out of fear, insecurities, and pride in order to achieve acceptance. They are always looking for man's affirmation, positions of power, and the applause of the crowds instead of the love of the Father. We must learn to do what we do because we love Him and nothing more.

Moses said in Exodus 33:18, "Show me Your glory"—not because he wanted to brag about it to his friends or impress the people, but rather because he loved the Lord with all of his heart. God revealed Himself to Moses; nothing was hidden or held back. Such is the case for us today. He gives us His glory and honor so that we could be one and the world would believe in Him.

Now when I speak of glory, I am not only talking about miracles, signs, and wonders, but I am also talking about attributes. Many have fallen in love with the gifts of power or revelation, but what about being like Him? Unity, compassion, mercy, and forgiveness are part of who He is.

We are so focused on what we want to do for Him that we forget to be like Him. God is not impressed with our actions; what impresses God is a humble, contrite spirit. What is uppermost for every believer is putting on the character of God.

I believe in miracles, and I believe that the world must

see a display of His glorious power, but more important than the miracles is the message. We represent the God of love, and our message should be a message of reconciliation, restoration, and revelation of His love. That is the glory that must be revealed to a hurting, broken world!

Now Where Is the Glory?

The glory of God is departing from our churches and our nation. Just as in the times of Eli (1 Sam. 3—4), the lamp of God is dimming all across America. Understand that the lamp was kept in the holy place where only the priest could enter and have communion with God. It was the place where the twelve loaves of bread were set at the table and the incense was burned, indicating a place of fellowship, substance, and light.

The light was dimming in this room because the priests had little time to enter into the presence of God. They had corrupted themselves and disobeyed God; they were too busy taking advantage of the people and were engaging in temple prostitution. They had no time for priestly duties or coming before God; they were too busy in the hustle of being in business, preoccupied with immorality, and trying very hard to be politically correct.

You see, they had too much to lose in obedience to be what they were called to be: the light of the world. Yet their secret sins caused them to have no public power; they were powerless, unable to stop the forces of darkness that were ravaging their land. They spoke a good word—but where was the power, the true anointing to hold back the devil and all his demons? The truth is that you can yell all you want in public and hold all the rallies and marches you desire, but if you are practicing secret sins, you have no power to influence, to bring about change, to impact your family or your community—much less the nation.

These priests abused their authority and led the people to sin (people follow their leaders) because they loved the darkness rather than the light. Their father Eli knew what they were doing, but he didn't have the courage to confront them, so he let them be. We are so afraid of losing relationships, positions, and people that we put up with it, turn a blind eye, and look the other away.

Where is the voice of the spiritual fathers in this hour? Spiritual fathers need not only to love, embrace, and affirm their children; they also need to confront, correct, and discipline those same children. A fatherless generation seeks affirmation, yet because of past negative experiences, they resist with passion the stern hand of a true, loving father.

Now when a critical problem arose for Israel, when they were confronted by a powerful enemy, they thought that if they had a service, brought the ark of the covenant, and yelled loud enough that everything would be alright (1 Sam. 4:1–6). Why is it that we, too, think that another conference, concert, or event will change anything? We think that if we bring in a top-tier preacher, major band or artist, and get the people shouting that the devil will flee. I've got news for you; the ark may be in the house, but the glory has already departed.

I grew up in a Pentecostal church, and we used to have some amazing services. We would jump, clap, run, and dance around the church for hours. But we failed to differentiate between that which was spiritual and that which was emotional. We deceived ourselves into thinking that we were right before God just because we had an upbeat, hell-stomping, hallelujah service. We would leave the church praising God, but by the time we got home, we had lost it. Perhaps on our way home somebody cut us off or maybe our car wouldn't start after we stopped at the grocery store to get some milk—or even worse, someone said something to us on the way out of church that really upset us.

Yet the truth is that we never lost anything, because we never had it. "It" was an emotional high, fed by our egos and sustained by our ignorance. Revival is not jumping, shouting, and falling onto the ground. Revival is much more than that. The glory of God is much more than that. The power of God must invade our very beings, causing us to run after God as our broken hearts cry out for more of Him.

The enemy had easy access into our lives, and he came and destroyed many of us because we fell in love with the Father's blessings and not with His majesty. Then, in our human wisdom, we reasoned that what we needed was another event, a conference, or revival services. Better yet, we added additional services and more church activities so that the people would not backslide. We became legalistic, demanding, and micromanaged people's lives, causing our children to run right into the hands of Satan.

Now please understand, there were times when we truly entered into His presence and saw His glory with signs and wonders, but for the most part we were naïve and had little discernment about how to steer a move of God in partnership with the Holy Spirit. Therefore, we could not discern between that which was emotional and that which was spiritual—and because of that, we also had a great loss of lives and ministries.

The same thing happened to the people of Israel; those poor people were slaughtered (30,000) because they didn't realize that the glory of God had already departed. Hear me when I say that we are about to lose our nation because we are too busy entertaining people instead of calling the nation to prayer, fasting, and repentance. It's about getting on our knees and repenting before the Lord so that a great awakening will come to America. America needs to be shaken, awakened, and revived! Our services cannot revolve around a run sheet; the only running we need to do is run into the presence of God.

We blame the politicians, the government, the elites, anyone and everyone, but the truth is that the glory of God is departing from this nation. It started in our churches, and now we see it in our nation. We are responsible for the condition of this nation because we allowed ourselves to be brought for a price; we allowed ourselves to be intimidated and stopped being the prophetic voice of God to the nation.

Yet there is a remnant, an army of men and women who are faceless and nameless. These people live for one purpose: to fulfill the mission of God. They are not necessarily Republicans or Democrats; they are not holding on to the fact that they may be black, white, Hispanic, or Asian; they understand that they are a multicultural, multiethnic army.

They have known the taste of rejection, the pain of abuse, and what it is to live in lack. But He has breathed life into them, and they are rising up and turning cities upside down. This is a praying army with extravagant worship that seeks to release the oil of unity in love with sign and wonders and acts of kindness across the land. And they are looking for you.

This multicultural prayer army consists of bishops, pastors, and leaders who have put aside their differences and have come together as one because they understand that unity provokes the supernatural—and when the supernatural is provoked, it invades the natural.

Every ministry has a particular sound, but when we come together to minister to God, we create an open heaven where the power of God is released.

Chapter Two
UNITY PROVOKES THE SUPERNATURAL

> After this I looked and a vast host appeared which no one could count, [gathered out] of every nation, from all tribes and peoples and languages. These stood before the throne and before the Lamb; they were attired in white robes, with palm branches in their hands. In loud voice they cried, saying, [Our] salvation is due to our God, Who is seated on the throne, and to the Lamb [to Them we owe our deliverance]! And all the angels were standing round the throne and round the elders [of the heavenly Sanhedrin] and the four living creatures, and they fell prostrate before the throne and worshiped God.
> —REVELATION 7:9–11, AMP

IN THIS SCRIPTURE we find a multitude in *one* place, with *one* mind, worshiping the Lord with *one* voice and causing the angels, the elders, and four living creatures to fall prostrate and join them in worshiping the King.

What caused heaven to react this way? I submit to you that it was unity. These people from different tribes and tongues were not focusing on their differences; they were focusing on the King. This is the model that we must seek; it is the strategy to overcome the enemy. This is the way of the Lord and the course the church must take to fulfill her destiny.

That independent spirit, that humanistic mindset must die at the foot of the cross. For too long we have modeled ourselves as a Samson that defeats the enemy all by himself instead of modeling Jesus as one who called His disciples friends and included them in what He did in spite of their limitations.

Our streets are covered in blood, our homes are being destroyed, and our anointing is but a flash in the pan because we fail to understand corporate destiny; we fail to understand that we must do this together as one body in Christ.

What will we do when we face our Master? What will we say when everything we have said has been written? America is dying, and the fault lies at the doorstep of the church because we are a church that is asleep and divided while our enemy is awake, united, and well prepared.

The prayer of Jesus, which has not been answered as of yet, is that we be one so that the world would believe. Unity provokes a sound from heaven; it releases the supernatural power of God into our natural atmosphere. The spiritual invades the physical, and miracles happen. Such is the power of the redeemed of the Lord—that we could call upon our mighty God with one voice and He would respond with a sound that would pierce the darkness and cause the gates of hell to tremble, for it knows what will follow.

Yet this specific sound can only be heard by those who understand that it is not the word *unity* that is important, but the sound created by unity. Just as on a piano, every key has its own sound, but it is not until they come together that a harmony is created that touches both heaven and earth. Every ministry has a particular sound, but when we come together to minister to God and man, we create an open heaven where the power of God is released as He responds to our sound with His own sound, creating a melody between us that brings transformation to all who hear it.

Therefore, it is important for us to understand that our unity creates a sound, and when heaven hears that sound, it responds, creating its own sound. That sound pierces the darkness as it invades the natural, and miracles happen—hence Pentecost comes.

> And when the day of Pentecost had fully come, they were all assembled together in one place, when suddenly there came a sound from heaven like the rushing of a violent tempest blast, and it filled the whole house in which they were sitting. And there appeared to them tongues resembling fire, which were separated and distributed and which settled on each one of them.
> —ACTS 2:1–3, AMP

On the day of Pentecost, they were in *one* place, in *one* accord, with *one* voice when suddenly a sound from heaven was heard, and all were filled with the Holy Ghost. Again I say to you, unity provokes the supernatural, and when the supernatural is provoked, it invades the natural.

Today there are many prayer warriors, intercessors, pastors, and visionaries that are crying out for transformational revival. They are hearing the sound of heaven, yet as a corporate body, we the church are not only not hearing it, but we are not understanding what little we might hear. We need to be set free from our own limited mindset and understand that it's a new season, a new day. For far too long we have been separated by cultural, economic, and language barriers, but no longer—because where the Spirit of the Lord is, there is freedom, and freedom has no barriers.

In the past, everything revolved around one anointed man or woman of God who would perform miracles and wonders in the name of Jesus. But today God is raising up a corporate body, an army that is releasing a corporate anointing that is far greater than one man or woman. This army is touching the nations with His love and giving them one more opportunity to see the King of glory. Individual destiny must embrace corporate destiny in this prophetic hour.

Unity will require you to lose your independence, which means no more superstars. You won't be the center of attention; they might not even mention your name or give you the recognition you feel you deserve. You will have to give up your agenda, your goals, and watch the crowds cheer for someone else. It will cost you to die to self and carry that humiliating cross everyday as you fight to be heard among the multiple voices that shout, "Thus says the Lord."

It is not until that moment when the glory of the Lord is risen upon you and you are allowed to speak that you realize that the glory and honor belongs to Him who died on the cross for you. You find yourself speechless and intimidated, not by devils or men, but by the fact that the almighty God has allowed you to speak in His name. What a responsibility, that a mere man or woman could be allowed to speak for the King of glory!

This reality causes me to accept the fact that I alone cannot have all of God's revelation for this fallen creation. It is a chorus of voices from anointed vessels that reveal

His majesty—one message released through many voices that speak and live as one, the power of unity!

If we would put away our competitive spirit and bury our differences, if we would unite under the banner of prayer and love, if we would cry out to God with one voice, I believe that He would hear us and heaven would have no other choice but to invade our natural world, bringing a revival such as the world has never seen before.

Let me remind you that the heavens were closed on the morning of Pentecost. Jesus had been crucified, and hell was busy celebrating its supposed victory. But there was a minor problem for the devil that he had yet to resolve. A small band of men and women were travailing in prayer in an upper room. There was an extravagant worship being released into the heavens by this group and a cry that caused the heavens to stand still. They saw the passion in these people and the will to unite in a sound, in a cry, that said, "Where is the God of Abraham, Isaac, and Jacob?"

It was the same cry that they had heard from the prophet Elijah so long ago, but now it was coming from one-hundred-and-twenty people who were corporately pulling on the hem of heaven, seeking that which seemed impossible to obtain. Heaven had no choice; it must respond, and respond it did. Fire came down, not on the sacrifice of an animal, but on men and women. Yes, men and women who decided to become a living sacrifice so that the glory of God could come down and transform their people.

One hundred and twenty became three thousand, which became hundreds of thousands, which became millions until they covered the entire world. When you provoke heaven with true worship, heaven must respond, and when heaven responds, miracles in our lives, family, communities, and nations will happen.

I believe that God longs to hear the cry of His people…once again. I challenge you to unite with your brother and your sister, and let us make a sound that would provoke the supernatural to respond with a sound from heaven that would invade our broken world and cause us all to live again.

This is why a group of bishops, pastors, and leaders from across the Mid-Atlantic region put aside their differences, tore down the walls that had divided them for too long, and have come together to form the Multicultural Prayer Army (movement), because we have come to understand that unity provokes the supernatural, and when the supernatural is provoked, it invades the natural.

As we look across this land, we see immorality, violence, and witchcraft embedded in our society. Our children are aborted and killed as we sacrifice to self; traditional marriage is being redefined for the benefit of those who think they know better than God; and our youth are being destroyed by the fallacy that they can do anything they want without consequences.

Just take a look at us. We walk around almost naked with clutched fists, cursing and mocking the God that created us. We are arrogant, blasphemous, and despicable people. There is a veil of darkness that covers our land, and now the prophets of God are beginning to be persecuted as Satan tries to kill our message by killing the messenger. But we will not be silent; no, this remnant will speak truth to power in the name of Jesus. And as we do that, we are also praying for America. Our prayer is "Holy Spirit, rain on our fields."

For America has become dry and barren as the desert;

people exist but do not live; and the hearts of men have become hard as stones. We cry out for rain to refresh our dry and thirsty souls because we love this nation, and we seek for her to return to her former glory. "America, America, God shed His grace on thee, and crown thy good with brotherhood from sea to shining sea!"

Saul was a rancher until he was anointed. He went from looking for donkeys to finding a kingdom that was looking for him.

Chapter Three
ANOINTING OIL

YOU HEARD THE bad news; now hear the good news. There is an anointing oil that God wants to pour over you! You're going to need it for the journey that lies before you. But before He releases that anointing oil over your life, I want you to understand what anointing oil is.

Anointing oil is the oil of crushed olives that was used to pour over the head of the priest. It was sprinkled on his garments as he was sanctified or separated for God's service. It was also the oil that was poured on the head of the king as he prepared to enter into a new level of authority to reign. The anointing oil symbolizes the Spirit of the Lord.

We have a clear example of this when Samuel took the vial of oil and poured it on David, and (the Scriptures say) the Spirit of the Lord came on him from that day forward. It is the oil of gladness (Ps. 45:7), which allows you to rejoice, even in troubled times. It is also the fresh oil (Ps. 92:10), which gives you a new, fresh beginning every day. The oil is used to anoint the sick so that they may be healed, and we know that this oil will never run dry. It reproduces and multiplies as your jar fills other vessels that are in desperate need of God's anointing.

This anointed oil can always be found in the dwelling place of the wise, yet the foolish never have enough of it. Their lamps keep going out, for they do not know how to travail in prayer. They easily fall asleep while waiting on the Master instead of moving under the anointing. The wise man knows that he needs the oil to grasp the Word of God and allow it to be a light unto his feet. The fool runs on emotions and soon gets discouraged; it doesn't take long before he runs dry, quits, and gives up.

David said: "You anoint my head with oil; my cup runs over" (Ps. 23:5). That is why he could say, "As the deer pants for the water brooks, so pants my soul for You, O God. My soul thirsts for God, for the living God" (Ps. 42:1–2).

The Lord has prepared a table for us, but we cannot sit down unless we are once again anointed. That is why we are being broken and going through immense trials; they are designed to push us into greatness. God is about to release an anointing in our lives in this prophetic hour, in the presence of our enemies, that will demonstrate to the entire world the power, mercy, and goodness of our God.

If ever we needed the anointing oil of gladness, it is now as we stand facing the winds of adversity in the middle of this dark night. Yet the joy of the Lord is our strength. We must believe God and rejoice. We must pray and sing in the middle of our prison and let the ground shake as the prison doors open and the chains fall off our hands.

Believe Him when He says, "Run after Me, and I will run after you." It is this encounter that will cause the sinner to stop in his tracks and contemplate the glory of our God in us. For when they see the anointing oil dripping down our beards, the garments with which He has dressed us, and the warmth of His love being released from us, they themselves will cry out, "The Lord is God! The Lord is God!" For not only will God revive our spirits, He will also revive our natural lives. And though we do not live for material things, God uses them to show us off and catch the eye of the unbeliever. He will take the treasures of the wicked and give them to us as a witness of His greatness. They will not be able to hold on to them, but when you and I possess them, our position will change. When your position changes, so will your condition. Understand that when you are anointed, your position changes; you are now kings and priests of the Most High.

Saul was a rancher like his natural father until he was anointed. While he was a rancher, he looked for donkeys, but when he met Samuel, he realized that a kingdom was looking for him. His only fault was that he could not grasp the grace of God; he corrupted his wisdom as he sought to please the people, and in the process, he disobeyed his God. That is a common problem for us, for God blesses us and lifts us up for all to see—and somehow, in our humanity, we forget that it was His grace and mercy that brought us this far. We start to think that we somehow built what we possess. Pride sets in, and we refuse to hear the voice of correction. It is but a matter of time before we start building altars to Baal and justifying our behavior as those who have now become enlightened or evolved into a new way of thinking.

He took us out of slavery, brought us through the desert, and took us into the Promised Land. Everyone is amazed because they thought we would die in Egypt, but we came out. They also assumed we would never make it through the desert, but we did. They swore we would never defeat the king of Jericho; we also did that. And our God gave us the city, its king, treasures, and men of valor.

But what have we done with that which He has given us? I will tell you what we have done. We have sat down, enjoyed the land and its riches, and fallen asleep, forgetting our divine purpose. He didn't give us all this just so we can sit around singing songs as we wait for His return. We are "a chosen generation, a royal priesthood, a holy nation, His own special people, that [we] may proclaim the praises of Him who called [us] out of darkness into His marvelous light" (1 Pet. 2:9)!

Let me tell you the story of the widow in 2 Kings 4:1–7. Her husband had been part of a group of prophets; he belonged to what we would call today a school of the prophets. He was a faithful servant who served God and dedicated himself to being trained. Yet he died, and his death caused a crisis for his widow. She didn't cause the crisis; her husband hadn't sinned. It was an economic problem, and she didn't know what to do about it.

There are things that happen to us through no fault of our own; perhaps something that happened years ago is now at our doorstep. You may have had nothing to do with it, but it's now taking your life and suffocating you. What do you do?

The widow went to Elisha, the man of God, with her complaint: "Your servant my husband is dead, and you know that your servant feared the LORD. And the creditor is coming to take my two sons to be his slaves" (2 Kings 4:1). Sometimes we get so consumed with our struggles that we lose sight of the fact that we no longer live; He lives inside of us (Gal. 2:20).

The man of God asked her if she had anything left in her house. Friend, I ask you, "What is left inside of you? After all your battles, distractions, trials, and tribulations, what's left inside of you?" The woman responded that she just had a jar of oil to light a small flame, something to anoint herself with before she died. My brother and sister, don't let your crying eyes deceive you; God has a plan for your little jar of oil. He is about to take you to a place you have never been before!

Elisha told the widow to find empty vessels—not a few, but many. He instructed her to pour out her jar of oil into empty vessels and God would take care of the rest. Here is a kingdom principle: when you pour yourself out into others, even the little that you have, will be multiplied and come back to you.

Pour the oil into those around you. Tell them your story, the things He has done for you. Awaken to the reality that you serve a mighty God. Release the oil and light up their lives. Anoint another life; release it, speak it, decree and command it. For God's sake, find another jar and pour your oil into it.

Listen, you have the Holy Spirit inside of you, and you have the Word of God in your heart. Therefore, if you have the Word inside of you, you have faith, and if you have faith, then you have power, and if you have power, you can speak the things that are not as though they were. Stop advertising doubt and stick to God's plan for your life.

We give the devil strategies on how to attack us by what comes out of our mouths. Stop advertising your weaknesses, your failures, and start talking about the mighty God you serve. You need to tell yourself, "I am what God says I am. And I can do what God says I can do, and I have what God says I can have!" It's called walking in miracles. Wherever you go, release the oil. It will break the curse and the yoke of bondage and poverty over the people you touch as well as yours. The oil will sustain you and renew you. There may be famine in the land, but you shall not die!

The world needs to see the glory of God. You and I

are a reflection of that glory. They must see Christ in us—not our agenda, position, or charisma. Remember, all of creation waits in eager expectation for the sons of God to be revealed. When you know who you are, what God has called you to do, and what God is capable of doing, you can decree and declare that which is not as though it was, because you have been anointed. The world is in a desperate state; entire nations are on the verge of collapse; and whether they know it or not, they are expecting something or someone to rescue them.

My dear brother and sister, we need fresh anointing oil over our lives, our cities, and our nations; we need a new beginning. So here is the good news, again. God is up to something big. There is an anointing oil that is about to be poured over all the nations; are you ready to see what you have never seen before? I am.

For too long we have called revival something that happens inside the four walls of our buildings. I seek an open heaven that will not only transform our churches, but also our communities, our cities, even our nation.

Chapter Four
AN OPEN HEAVEN

We have been called to unity by none other than Jesus Christ Himself. We have been anointed with oil, crowned with power and authority to reign and sit with Him in high places, and we have been called to open the heavens.

Now, there are numerous places in the Bible where we read about an open heaven. But I want to focus on John 1:50–51: "Jesus answered and said to him, 'Because I said this to you, "I saw you under the fig tree," do you believe? You will see greater things than these.' And He said to him, 'Most assuredly, I say to you, hereafter you shall see heaven open, and the angels of God ascending and descending upon the Son of Man.'"

Notice that in verse 50, Jesus said, "You will see greater things than these." He continued to tell Nathanael in verse 51 that he will see an open heaven and angels ascending and descending upon the Son of man.

The question we have to ask is this: "What was God referring to in these verses?" I can tell you this much; God was referring to much more than healings or prophetic utterances. He was saying that Nathanael would see what it means for God to dwell among His people. We need to keep in mind that the raising of the dead, the opening of blind eyes, and the healing of the lame are just the fruit of God's presence being manifested and released upon His people here on Earth. We need more than just a healing crusade in some part of a city; we need to see heaven here on Earth being released by us as we commit to serve and interact with our communities.

Our model is the early church. It had unity, love, and the power to turn entire cities upside down. The presence of God filled the believers; in other words, God was in them, producing miracles and releasing His presence (love) on the people they lived among. That is an open heaven. I get frustrated when I hear so many people say there is an open heaven in their church just because they are seeing miracles take place. Believe me when I say I am happy to see and hear about miracles taking place. But I seek more than that; I seek to see transformation that is not only taking place in our churches, but in our communities, in our cities, and in our nations.

For too long we have called revival something that happens inside the four walls of our building. We feel good, services last for hours, miracles do take place, and when we leave church, we tell all of our brothers and sisters that our church is in revival. In the meantime, we pass by the homeless on the way to church, make sure the security system is on in our cars because we don't want it to get stolen while we are in church, and look down at the prostitute who is standing on the street corner right next to our church.

If souls are not being saved, if our community is not being changed, if there are no acts of kindness found in our hearts for the broken and needy, then—well, I hate to tell you this—but what you have is not a revival or an open heaven; it is simply a nice blessing from the Lord. I want more than blessings; I want His presence in my life, home, and community.

The other thing we do as a church is withdraw behind our four walls when the world starts to press in. Today the world is pushing open the doors of the church by making laws and establishing belief systems that go against the Word of God. They are now coming into the church and enforcing those laws.

In the meantime, as we try to survive, Scripture is twitted and new boundaries are set. Truth has become relative; everybody has their own version of truth, and the church wanders in circles waiting for the rapture instead of being the salt of the Earth. If the heavens can be opened, then it also means they can also be closed:

> When I shut up heaven and there is no rain, or command the locusts to devour the land, or send pestilence among My people...
> —2 Chronicles 7:13

It is clear that God not only can open the heavens, but also close them. Now when the heavens are closed, evil floods the land; darkness increases; and the devil comes to kill, steal, and destroy. Drought, floods, earthquakes, and the cost of living increases. All of these things bring stress, anxiety, and depression upon the people. The purity of the children is lost, faith cannot be found, and pornography and immorality plague the nations.

Now let us look at the condition of our nation and come to the obvious conclusion that the heavens are closed over our nation and that we desperately need an awakening to take place. Our national leaders, the elites of our nation, profess that they are evolving, and they convince the masses to follow their path to destruction. They invest billions upon billions to convince us to follow them; from

Hollywood to your local media outlet, they inject their lies into the heart of our children.

The Bible tells us the story of a man named Tobiah. He was an enemy of Nehemiah who tried to stop the work of rebuilding the walls of Jerusalem. When Nehemiah was out of the city, Eliashib prepared a room for Tobiah in the courts of the house of God. When Nehemiah came back, he found Tobiah in the house. He was so angry that he took all of Tobiah's things and threw them out of the room (Neh. 13:6–8).

Today, Tobiah is in our homes as well, and we don't know it. He has come in through our television set, iPhones, video games, and movies, and he (the devil) is corrupting our children and youth. All of this is birthed from a perverted heart and a corrupted wisdom that believes it knows more than the God who created it. Today, our children play with toys that come with a personality, and thus they act out what they see on television. They learn witchcraft, immorality, and violence as they act out the personalities they have seen, and we purchased these toys for them.

We can spend eternity blaming the elites of this nation, yet we must also accept responsibility for not living up to the covenant we have with God. The sins of the priests cannot be ignored, for surely we too have corrupted ourselves and allowed the whispers of Satan ("Has God indeed said...?" Gen. 3:1) to manipulate us. Our faces are no longer buried in the ground in worship, nor are our knees bent in prayer and reverence to Him who took us out of slavery and gave us the nations as inheritance. Now we have no power in our message, no light (presence) in our house, and no influence to lead our families (much less the nation) back to God.

We must first repent, and then be healed; then and only then will we be able to stand in the gap and cry out for the heavens to be opened over our nation. We must cry out to the one who closed the heavens. We need to go to the Father, seek His face, and ask Him to open the heavens once again so that the fire of His glory will cover the land.

Before we can use authority against the enemy, we need to go to the one we have offended in the first place, and with a heart of humility and a spirit of repentance ask for forgiveness. We need the heavens to open up and the light of His glory to shine through. Because darkness has come and deception is its companion, together they have caused us to fall away as they have covered our eyes with layer upon layer of darkness. Lord, help us see!

Yet those of us who believe and have been awakened must walk in humility and not act as if we are the only ones chosen to confront and correct. In every city, there are fathers who are gatekeepers over regions who must be respected and honored. We are not called to confront but to partner with others. And, if for some reason, they do not care to partner with us or even hear us, we need to seek their blessing as we enter into their God-given region.

Too many times I have seen major ministries come into a city and never ask the gatekeepers of that city permission to enter. They host events in stadiums or arenas, and most of those who attend come from outside of the city. They never touch the city; neither do you see representation from within the city in these events. The fathers feel disrespected, and they don't support the events. All the while, the devil is rejoicing with the division that has been created within the church.

As my dear friend Doug Stringer so eloquently puts

it, from preachers to politicians, we need a revival of character. God has always wanted to dwell with man. *Emmanuel* means "God with us." We lost that privilege as a veil of darkness has covered all the nations—but in this darkness, we have learned that if we build an altar of prayer and place on it a sacrifice of praise, the heavens will open.

I cannot help but remember how Elijah rebuilt the altar, that meeting place of God. He placed on it a sacrifice and cried out to heaven; heaven responded by piercing the darkness, and holy fire came down. We must do the same.

Genesis tells us the story of Jacob, how he deceived his brother, stole his birthright, and was forced to run for his life as his brother sought his revenge (Gen. 28:1–13). Yet in that process he came to a place he did not know; it was night, and he was tired. So he took a stone, made it into a pillow, and fell asleep.

What he did not know was that this place was an open heaven. In his dream, he saw a ladder with angels going up and down. He had stumbled into a place he would later call the house of God. There God spoke to him: "I am with you; I will keep you. I will go with you, bring you back, and never leave you until everything I have spoken over you becomes true."

We need to awaken from our dream, raise our voices, and praise Him, for God is waiting for us to stand in that place where Abraham (our spiritual fathers) had already praised, sacrificed, and sealed as holy ground. You see, what Jacob did not know was that this ground had already been stamped as holy by his own grandfather when he first entered the land.

I am trying to tell you that someone has already planted and sealed this land for our God! Those who discovered this country dedicated it to the Lord with sweat, blood, and tears. God is just looking for someone to stand in the right place, in the gap, and say the same things God is saying so that the heavens can once again be open and humanity can have one last chance before the end.

Does not your heart burn with passion to see the glory of God be manifested in this hour? We need rain like fire to fall from heaven, breaking the yoke that Satan has had over the people. Immorality, violence, hate, depression, and so many other things will be burnt by the fire of His glory coming down like rain.

It starts with prayer, but it doesn't finish there. We also need action, for a dream without a strategy and a timeline is but an illusion. As bishops, pastors, and leaders, it seems we don't have time for anything anymore. The years go by, and when we come to realize it, we have no strength left to fulfill our God-given dream. We got too distracted with things to do and people who just take up our time with foolishness. I can't sit around any longer; I've got to get up and do what I was born to do.

Jacob woke up and realized that God was in that place; he just didn't know it. God was in the darkness, for darkness is not darkness for Him (Ps. 139:12). God was in the darkness waiting for Jacob to arrive so He could show him that even in the dead of the night the gate of heaven was still open for him.

Oh, how I pray that we might not only confess our sins in humility with travailing prayer, but overcome our differences in love and worship Him extravagantly so that the heavens would open up and the world would see the glory of our God one last time.

In your moment of conflict, you must not speak your own words because they will demand justice. Replace your words with His and understand that suffering is part of your call.

Chapter Five
THE BATTLE THAT IS BEFORE US

MAKE NO MISTAKE about it: the moment you go to a new level of anointing, the enemy will come against you. Anger follows promotion, and if God has called you for greatness in this prophetic hour (which I believe He has), then you have been promoted. There is something about a righteous man or woman that draws the anger of Satan. The devil hates faithfulness; he hates it when you run after God, and he hates that God would use such a fragile human being to defeat his army.

When your position changes, your condition will also change; therefore, you must ask God to change your heart so you are able to walk in this new anointing. When Saul met Samuel, God had to change his heart (1 Sam. 10:9). He went from having a rancher's heart to having a king's heart. As long as you have a rancher's heart, you will not go beyond those limitations. Remember, kings possessed lands and not just territories.

The moment the Philistines heard the news that David had become king; they went out in full force to capture him. But God was protecting David and allowed the enemy's plans to be revealed to him. David was no fool; he sought out the Lord, and God gave him a plan to defeat the Philistines. He defeated the Philistines in Baal Perazim, which means "god of divisions." In that battle, the Lord divided the pure from the impure as He destroyed the gods of the Philistines as water that breaks out. In the same manner, God will give us the victory over our enemies!

Even so, we need to understand and accept the fact that, while some of us may be rescued and obtain great victories in a supernatural fashion, others will simply perish as martyrs for the cause. I always get a kick out of how many preachers love to preach about Peter being freed from jail (Acts 12), but never mention the death of James the brother of John in a single sentence.

We need to accept the fact that, as Christians, many are and will be persecuted, cast in jail, and even killed for the gospel. Many of us in the Western world don't believe that this will ever happen to us; we need to wake up. Christians will be and are being persecuted in America. Goliath has stepped out of the shadows and is challenging the church of Jesus Christ.

Stephen was full of faith and power; he did great signs and wonders (Acts 6:8–15). But there arose some who, having failed to resist him, now wanted to kill him. Not only did they stir up the people, they were able to get the leadership involved, and soon he was arrested. At the trial, truth prevailed, but truth didn't help Stephen because they refused to hear it. Just because the truth comes out, and you are right, doesn't mean you will get justice. Today we have judges that legislate from the bench—immoral, secular humanist judges that are persecuting Christians any way they can.

Stephen was taken out of the city and stoned as everyone rejoiced. The mistake the devil made was to allow those who stoned Stephen to place their clothing at the feet of Saul. He should have known that there would be a transfer of anointing taking place. When their clothes, which carried Stephen's DNA, touched Saul, a transfer took place. You see, my personal opinion is that even though they took off their outer clothing so as not to get them stained with Stephen's blood, his DNA was already on them; his blood was already on them to some degree. Like the bones of Elisha, like Peter's shadow and Elijah's mantle, a transfer took place. Stephen's blood on those clothes carried a great anointing because spilled blood speaks. It still prays, and it still believes. Abel's blood cried out for justice while Stephen's blood cried out for mercy; they both spoke from the ground.

They may reject you, stone you, and count you as dead. Yet you still shall live. You may die in the memory of men, but God will rise you up again. For His Word says, "If a man dies, shall he live again?" (Job 14:14). In your moment of conflict, when stones are being cast at you from all directions, you must allow yourself to cry out His Word within you. Stephen cried, "Lord, do not charge them with this sin" (Acts 7:60). What do you do when He allows you to be slain? You kneel down, cry out, and let your blood speak.

Now here is the key to all of this: you cannot speak your words because your words will demand justice (think of Abel), and your words will bring with them discouragement and poison. Your words reveal your true spiritual condition and what is inside of you, including your poverty and bitterness. You must remove your words and replace them with His Word. This can only happen when there is true brokenness.

Our destiny awaits us, yet we cannot reach it because, in spite of all the preaching, shouting, and jumping we do, His Word has not replaced ours. But when His Word is inside of us, it will come out as living waters even when we are pierced as Christ was, releasing blood and water. Then the world will know that you are a man or a woman of God.

I learned something some time ago, and that is that all great leaders must suffer much. The call upon their lives is so great it requires a thorn in the flesh to keep them from becoming proud. There is a particular cross that they must bear, a divine process that will make them highly effective warriors. The more they cry, "Take it away," the more the Lord will tell them, "My grace is all you need." That is why when Paul boasted; he didn't brag about seeing paradise; rather, he bragged about his weaknesses so that the power of Christ could rest on him. Three times he begged the Lord to take the thorn away, and God replied, "My power works best in weakness" (see 2 Cor. 12:9).

Have you ever begged God to do the same thing? Have you ever taken pleasure in insults, hardships, persecution, and troubles? Paul did, and because he did, God manifested His power through him. He learned to run toward God in his moment of pain and never depend upon his humanity for strength or wisdom. It is in the presence of God that we find strength, faith, and anointing to press forward in our journey. It is also in His presence that we find healing, and believe me, the church today needs healing.

When you are being attacked and persecuted, you get hurt. For many of us, it seems like we have been getting hurt all of our lives. I grew up on the streets of New York City, in foster care and state institutions, and when I came to Christ, I thought all my hurts would be healed and my pain would go away. And though that was true, what I didn't know was that I was going to be hurt in the house of my Father.

Church folk can be truly mean people. We don't do a great job representing the one who saved us. The truth is that we have been so abused, rejected, and abandoned, among other things, that we hurt even those who are trying to help us. People will turn on you in an instant when that which is inside of them comes out when it is least expected. Those kinds of hurts only Jesus can heal.

Hurting Christians can't tell the difference between abuse and discipline; they often confuse the firm hand of a loving father with the whip of the abuser. I see so many seeking affirmation from a brother or a sister; I see them living insecure lives and misunderstanding even the smallest thing people tell them.

Don't expect your brother to do what only Jesus can do. Only He can heal the brokenhearted and bind up their wounds (Ps. 147:3). It was David who said, "O LORD my God, I cried out to You, and You healed me" (Ps. 30:2) We should do the same. Just be the hands of Jesus and allow yourself to heal the brokenhearted.

We must conclude that persecution will come from within and from without. Do not be afraid of the one who kills the body, for even if that occurs, your bones will testify of His glory, and His resurrection power will be manifested for all to see in the coming days. You must not, however, let bitterness take hold of your heart; understand that all of this is designed to make you into the image of Christ. Never lose hope; He is coming back.

In the meantime, let us settle this in our souls: whether I live or die, it will be for His glory. And if and when I die, my blood will reach out, touch a Saul, and turn him into a Paul.

Never submit to a political or religious agenda. You have another agenda, the agenda of the King. Stand firm in love and don't allow yourself to be intimidated by those who surround you.

Chapter Six
SPEAKING TRUTH TO POWER

On April 27, 2015, the city of Baltimore prepared to lay to rest the body of Freddie Gray. Freddie had died of injuries he suffered while he was in police custody. This event followed numerous incidents that minority groups had had with police in Ferguson, Missouri, and New York City. Protestors took to the streets, and what was supposed to be a peaceful march soon turned into a full-fledged riot with multiple incidents of fires and looting taking place. People were arrested, police officers were injured, and politicians convened at City Hall trying to get a handle on all of it. The mayor imposed a curfew, and the National Guard was deployed—all in an attempt to keep the peace.

I had attended the funeral service and was still in my office in my clergy attire that afternoon when I received a text from a high-ranking police officer asking all clergy to please go to Pennsylvania and North Avenue because people were throwing bottles of water and rocks at police there. It was his hope that, as peacemakers, we could calm the crowd down and help restore order.

Immediately, I jumped in my car and went to the location. After parking my car, I got out and started to walk toward the location that had been indicated to me. As I approached Pennsylvania Avenue, I got the feeling that I was walking into a war zone. Police cars had been destroyed and set on fire, a pharmacy was also set on fire, and debris covered the streets.

When I reached the corner of Pennsylvania and North Avenue, I saw police officers in riot gear with shields yelling at the crowd, "Step back! Step back!" About thirty to fifty feet in front of them were a couple of hundred people, yelling back at them, throwing all kind of things at them. I, in turn, found myself standing alone between the police and the rioters. I literally ended up standing on ground zero, and before I knew it, I was covered in smoke and either pepper spray or tear gas. I really don't know. But what could I do? Hundreds of people were yelling, police sirens blowing, fires burning, and police officers banging their shields ordering everyone back. What could one preacher do? Nothing!

Yet, I knew that greater was He that was inside of me than that which was all around me. So, I stood my ground. I took a stand for Jesus and prayed. I prayed that His glory would shine through me and somehow reach all those around me.

A youth leader from another church who had recognized me, joined me, and together we moved around the protesters and rioters praying and crying out for our city. To my surprise, protesters started coming up to me, shaking my hand, and thanking me for being there. No one hurt me; they simply thanked me and asked for prayer.

CNN reporters were also there, reporting live the events as they were happening. As the camera swung around, they caught me in the picture and it went viral. In a matter of minutes, I was getting phone calls and text messages from around the country. Most wanted me to get out—including the youth leader that was with me—especially after a young man pulled out a large knife and twice punctured the water hose that the fire department had set up in hopes of turning off the fire that was burning in the pharmacy.

That day alone 200 people were arrested, and 144 cars and 15 buildings were destroyed by fire. In addition to this, close to 150 police officers were injured as the city exploded in violence and looting. For the first time in Major League Baseball history, a game was played that was closed to the public. Truly, Baltimore had lived up to its name of being a city of firsts.

Unfortunately, the violence did not stop after the riots. As of August of this year (2015), our city has recorded more murders than in all of 2014. It seems as though hell has swept in and is ravaging our city. The question is why?

I have two important observations that I would like to share with you. The first concerns hopelessness. As a society, we have to understand that this was more than the death of one young man. We must look beyond what the media presents and what politicians or those so-called professionals that end up being interviewed on our nightly news say.

This is a generation of hurting, broken people who have lost all hope and trust no one. They have no dreams and no vision for the future; they exist but do not live. For years, these people have lived in poverty and in injustice. They have been abused by a system that is supposed to protect them, abandoned in the hood with no education, depending on a handout from the government that basically trapped them with the illusion that it can help. No government can heal a broken heart.

The truth is that no amount of money or programs can solve this dilemma. We have spent 22 trillion dollars trying to eradicate poverty with little to nothing to show for it. Our cities are crime-infested; our streets are covered in blood. No wonder they cry out, "No justice, no peace!"

What do you do when hope and faith is lost? I can answer that because I was there. I have lived the life of those rioters. My mother died when I was eight-and-a-half years old, my father had abandoned our home before I was born, and I grew up on the streets of New York City, moving from foster home to foster home, from state institution to state institution. I hated the police, the system, and anyone in authority. Why? Because I was abused by those in authority—from the house parent in the foster home, to police brutality, to politicians promising much but doing very little. I can speak because I sat where they sit.

The answer to the crisis in Ferguson, New York City, Philadelphia, and Baltimore is not more programs or more money for this or that. The answer for a hurting heart is love…the love of God expressed through the hands of a follower of Christ who has truly been moved to compassion by that which he himself has experienced. The power of that love, expressed by acts of kindness, will eventually win the hearts of angry, untrusting, hurting people. This will open the door for them to receive instruction, correction, restoration, and wholeness. It will allow each person to live again. You see, someone loved me even when I spat in their face, when I betrayed their confidence, and when I stole from them. They kept on loving me until I saw God in their face and dared to believe.

This is the ministry of the church. But we have been too busy getting in bed with politicians, building our kingdoms, and believing our own commercials. We are really good at talking, but really bad at doing. We don't evangelize or disciple anymore; we are too busy entertaining the people instead of doing real ministry. And now the cries of anger can be heard across the land. No one wants to hear a message of doom. Yet my message is not of doom, but of the greatest opportunity the church has had since Pentecost! I'm talking about a season of reformation, restoration, and awakening.

We must get off the beach and stop the party; we must stop running after fame and fortune. We must run after the lost, the broken, and the hurting. We been called to set the captive free, mend the broken heart, and let America see the light of His glory once again. Somewhere out there is a little girl crying, an abused wife living in fear, an angry young man bent on violence, and a father who lives in shame. What they all need now is the love of the Father, in action, so they can see Him in all His glory through you and me, and thus be saved.

My second observation regards the corruption of our political leadership. I am talking about those that are in power in Washington, DC, and all across this nation. Never in the history of our nation have we seen so many political leaders turn their backs on God. When you confront them, they say they have evolved, are enlightened, and no longer have a need for religion in the public square. They accuse you of being close-minded, call you a bigot, and challenge your interpretation of the Bible. I wonder what the founding fathers would say about that. They have led the nation into sin and pushed God out. They have removed the Ten Commandments from the court houses, pictures of Jesus from schools and universities, the Bible from hotel rooms, and placed a demand on Christian clergy not to pray in His name.

I remember when I was first invited to pray at City Hall here in Baltimore. I was sent a letter giving me instructions on how I should pray and was told not to pray in the name of Jesus because I would offend others in the room. Well, I was offended. How can you ask me not to pray in His name? Does invoking His name under the anointing of the Holy Spirit somehow trouble your spirit? Does it cause you to cover your ears?

I threw the letter away, marched down to City Hall, and prayed my heart out in the name of Jesus. Then I told them, "If you don't want me to pray in the name of my Savior, don't invite me back. But I will never submit to your political agenda. I have another agenda, the agenda of the King." I also got tired of politicians coming to my church on election year, but never appearing again until the next election. They would come, quote the same scriptures, tell the same stories, and make the same promises that they never kept. They would kiss our babies, smile for the camera, and then ask you to please vote for them. After you voted for them, they would turn around and introduce legislation that is contrary to our beliefs—and we still keep voting them in time and time again. No more; wake up church! They lie to your face and manipulate the people with half-truths. I said this once in a press conference, and I will say it again: I have seen gangs in the streets of New York City, Baltimore, and elsewhere. But I have never seen the kind of gangs that sit in the seats of power, who claim to represent the people, when in truth all they are interested in doing is maintaining their power at any cost. Their power has corrupted them, their ambition has blinded them, and they will stop at nothing to fulfill their own agenda.

A politician such as a mayor holds the keys to a city. They are delegated authorities that can bless or destroy the city. They are gatekeepers, and if they open the gate of the city to evil, evil will come in and destroy it. This is what happens when those in authority push God out of the city, region, or nation; you are left with no protection. Your women are raped, children abused, homes destroyed, and violence and immorality sit at your dinner table. The wise have become utter fools; now the nation is on fire, and they can't control or stop it. Everyone does what he or she pleases, there is no order, and police officers are being targeted, shot, and killed. They are our only protection from the criminals that are running in our streets—all because those in leadership have pushed God out, unlocked the gates, and allowed Satan in.

Consider this, for example: Our mayor officiated a mass wedding of gay and lesbian couples at Druid Hill Park on June 15 in 2013 (Father's Day weekend). She also served as grand marshal in their festival and has been open in her support of gay rights. What she did not realized was that she opened a gate that allowed greater evil to come into our city. During this same time, many in the church and around the world had been praying for the city of Baltimore. We were pushing darkness back, and crime was going down to historic levels. Murder rates had also gone down, and there was a great outpouring of service in the community. We were excited at the transformation that was taking place.

But then our governor (who wants to be president) and our mayor pushed their agenda forward and pushed the church out. They found preachers that would agree with them and spent millions of dollars to push through same-sex marriage in Maryland. They succeeded and celebrated their victory. These are the same politicians that quoted the Bible and say they are Christians, yet they have violated the very Word of God—the one they placed their hand on and swore to uphold. Please note that I am not judging their salvation, but rather their actions. The Bible tells me that by their fruits you will know them.

The same thing is true of our president, Barack Obama. No sooner had the Supreme Court made its decision on same-sex marriage than he covered the White House with the rainbow colors of the LGBT community. Again, don't get me wrong. I have met the president personally and have been with Michele Obama at the White House. They are really incredible people, but someone has been speaking into their ears, and it isn't a Spirit-filled believer. We need men and women of prayer that surround the president because there are many things happening behind the scene that you simply don't know about.

Decisions have been made, and agreements have been signed that are changing the course of this nation. Never forget that there are consequences to our actions; as you look around this nation, you are seeing things that have never happened before. We see fires that behave as if they have a life of their own, burning everything before them; tornados and hurricanes destroying large areas of our land; historic droughts parching regions; etc. Again I say, nature is screaming, yet no one is listening.

The philosophical man, the elites of this nation, the humanist, and the scientist will all tell you that it is global warming, that some strange phenomenon has happened, or that there is a scientific explanation for it. All have forgotten to read their Bibles and to seek revelation and understanding of what is really taking place.

All over this nation, people are tired of hurting. They are tired of the injustice that they see. From California to New York, they protest; they cry out in anger because our leadership has failed us. Yet our leadership walks around like the emperor who was made a fool of by two swindlers that convinced him to walk naked beneath a canopy in a procession as all the people congratulated him on his new clothing. It took a small child to say, "But he doesn't have anything on!" for him to realize his true condition. Even then, he pressed forward with the procession. Good Lord, let us hear the voice of the prophet.

We have become a nation that flaunts its immorality in God's face with no regard for the fact that He is the creator and we are the created. We have gone from fornication, to common-law marriages, to no-fault divorce, to adultery, incest, pornography, same-sex marriages, and now transgenderism. Truly, we have evolved; we have become gods in our own minds with no need of a sovereign God. We have created our very own Frankenstein. But we still have hope for America, for there is a remnant, a multicultural, multiethnic prayer (movement) army that has been called to speak truth to power—and speak that truth in love.

Throughout my life, I have been blessed to have met many politicians. Truth be known, there are some good people out there serving our communities. You may not agree with everything they do, but many do love and serve this country. Let me be very clear: not all politicians are bad. The church at times has walked away from them; we don't pray for them; we don't pray for the nation. We complain, but we don't minister to them. These intelligent, gifted people know law, policy, and procedural order. But many know very little about the Word of God, intimacy with the Him, or being in His presence. They have never stepped into the fullness of the Holy Spirit.

It's our job to speak into their lives, to prophesy, and to love them unconditionally. To have a true transformation of a nation, we need to reach the elites of the nation. We have got to find those people that are in positions of power; CEOs of major corporations, billionaires, millionaires, and politicians. Pray that God would open a door that no one can shut, so that you can walk in and reach those who at the end of it all truly hope that there is a God who loves them unconditionally. We must speak truth to power and see America come back to Jesus!

Note: We also need to get more Christians leader into politics and support the ones that are already there.

The journey of transformation begins by seeing yourself from God's perspective. He knows everything about you—the good, the bad, even the ugly—and yet He still wants you. Think about that!

Chapter Seven
CHANGE OF MIND

We were born with a divine purpose. That purpose comes with promises for our own good. He has promised us and has prepared for us great things. Therefore, we stand in expectation, waiting to see what our mighty God is about to do. However, when we look across the spectrum, our hearts get heavy as we see the destruction of the land and its people. We wonder, in private, why the promises of God are not coming to pass. We have read the Word and heard the prophecies, yet time goes on, and we do not see the fulfillment of that which was spoken into our lives and community. Faith begins to fail us, and discouragement gets hold of our hearts. But I believe that the problem is not in God; I believe the problem has to do with us. I believe that we do not see fulfillment in our personal lives and in community because of the way we think about and see things.

Allow me to explain. Moses put twelve men in a room; all were facing the same situation, and all saw the same thing. Ten said; "It is impossible; we can't do it," while two said, "It's possible; we can do it!" (Num 13:26–14:9). Whenever you look at something with a defeated mindset, you are already defeated—even before the battle begins—because of the way you see things. Most of the time we make it (or not), based not on what is happening, but on how we see what is happening. The victim mentality has such a hold on us that even our eyesight is affected; we can't see what God sees.

Elisha's servant could not see what surrounded him. He only saw his enemies, and his heart dropped. It caused him to panic and run. Fear paralyzed him, and he was defeated even before one arrow was launched. Thus, Elisha was forced to pray for his eyes because he could not see what the prophet was seeing (2 Kings 6:14–17).

We always battle with sight. The ten spies saw themselves as grasshoppers. The result was that they not only delayed God's purposes for His people, but their destiny was destroyed. They simply could not see, and their inability to see caused them to die in the wilderness. The problem is not with God; it is with us and our inability to see what He sees.

Our perception of ourselves is based on our experiences from the past. Our hurts, the baggage we carry, and our insecurities (among other things) all lead us to a dead end. The fact that many of us are not capable of or willing to make the necessary changes, in my opinion, is the primary reason we do not obtain that which has been prepared for us. We are stubborn people, bound by a religious, legalistic spirit that keeps us enslaved in fear. We play the blame game, and we blame the system, the cops, our parents, and the pastor, etc. Yet God has never fulfilled His purposes by depending on man's system. He is God; He operates outside of the system of this world. He is not limited by the police, politicians, or clergy. His will is accomplished regardless of what people do to you and me. We, therefore, must believe and act upon His Word. Faith requires action; it requires obedience. Will He find faith when He returns?

To see like Christ, you need a change of mind. Listen,

your talents are diminished because of the way you think. Your strength is weakened, and your destiny is delayed because of the way you think. God wants to change that!

> Don't copy the behavior and customs of this world, but let God transform you into a new person by changing the way you think. Then you will learn to know God's will for you, which is good and pleasing and perfect.
> —Romans 12:2, NLT

Because of the way we think, we are distracted, distressed, and preoccupied. Instruction is difficult to receive, discipline is irritating, and correction is an offence because we think as men instead of as sons of God. The devil is focused on our minds; he wants our minds because they are very powerful.

The mind takes in information, focuses on that information, and creates a feeling that pushes us to take action. If Satan can keep you focused on your past, a problem, or a situation and get you to take action based on that, he will lead you to a false future, instead of the future God has prepared for you. True change will never come, Christianity will become a frustration, and you will end up becoming useless for the kingdom of God. You will run from one event to another, from one concert to another, from one conference to another always looking for that magic formula that will fulfill you and birth the promise that was given to you. The truth is that events can never truly give you lasting results; those are only obtained in the presence of the King.

The journey of transformation begins by seeing yourself from God's perspective. He thought so much about you that He sent His Son Jesus Christ to save you. He thought so much about you that He is preparing a place in heaven for you. As a matter of fact, He thought so much about you that He made you His son, His daughter—think about that. God knows everything about you, the good, the bad, even the ugly, and yet He still wants you!

The battle is therefore within us and concerns how we define ourselves. We allow the enemy to define us, and we give him strategies on how to attack us by what comes out of our mouths. Stop putting yourself down, stop telling hell your weaknesses, and for the love of God, stop confessing and taking ownership of all the lies that have been spoken over your life. Whose report will you believe?

Our minds can only be changed when we stop listening to and imitating the behavior and customs of the world. Human reasoning is not sufficient to discern that which is good or bad. To make proper decisions, we need the Holy Spirit and the Word of God. In short, we need to think like Him. The world is waiting for the manifestation of the sons of God, but we cannot be revealed without a new mind that thinks and acts as He does.

I believe that God thinks in terms of His kingdom. In other words, I believe He seeks to build His kingdom in our lives and in the lives of those He has set free. To me, that is transformation and revival. But for too many in the church, revival is a weekend rally where we invite a speaker to come, minister to us, see a few folks get healed, and conclude with a celebration of some sort. No change, no souls being saved, and no transformation of our community.

The word *revival* means to live again, to rekindle into a flame the spark which was nearly extinguished. It relates to those who are Christians yet need to be revived. It is more than renewal and more than a blessing. However, we kind of get stuck on this.

For me, revival has to do with preparing the Earth for the return of our Lord and Savior Jesus Christ. For me, this must include salvations, community transformation, and entire regions awakening to the power of His love. Allow me to bring greater clarification: historians tell us that John the Baptist brought nearly one million people to a baptism of repentance. After him, Jesus came preaching that the kingdom of heaven was at hand. Yet for all the multitudes, miracles, and signs and wonders, Jesus lamented over Jerusalem. He wept because they failed to recognize the time of their visitation. They could not perceive that God had come and prophecy was being fulfilled. They ended up turning against their own Savior.

How could they miss it? They missed it because when God visits His people, He seeks two things. He first seeks to destroy the works of the devil and second to build His kingdom. He did not come to revive us so we can go back to being the way we were. He saved and revived us so He could transform us into His image. He set us free so that He could empower us to rebuild, rise up, and repair the breach. He sent us to make disciples and prepare the nations for His return.

The very moment God removes our burdens, He also removes our excuses. Now that you are free from oppression, the Lord expects you to put aside your differences, unite with your brother and sister, and begin to transform our world for Christ. This is the mind of Christ. Therefore, when we cry out for revival, we are crying for God's kingdom to reign on Earth as it is in heaven. Yet for this to happen, we must truly surrender to His will and ways.

We need more than a visitation; we need habitation, and we need transformation.

Listen, our homes are being destroyed, our streets are full of homeless people, and our mental institutions are filled with people hearing voices. Our youth are killing each other, our children are being raped and abused, and every day the cost of living keeps getting worse and worse. What bothers me most is that church folk just want to sing, clap, jump, and sit around waiting for His return while the world is going to hell in a handbasket. Never forget that we are call to be the light of the world. We have been called to turn cities upside down, to preach the gospel, and to serve in love those who live in darkness.

We need a change of mind so that we can rise up, go out, and set somebody free. What kind of revival do we really want? I know this much, I don't want God to say to me, "You missed it!" I want Him to say, "Well done, My good and faithful servant!" For that to happen I need a change of mind.

Heaven is waiting to hear the cry of God's people. We must cry out, "Your kingdom come. Your will be done on earth as it is in heaven" (Matt. 6:10). When God's people return to prayer, when we pray at home, in church, and at the marketplace, the heavens will open up, and fire will come down, piercing the darkness that has consumed us. Then the nation shall see the glory of God once again before the end, and they will have their final opportunity to fall down on their knees and cry out, "The Lord is God! The Lord is God!"

In review, there are different kinds of revivals. I seek not only the transformation of the Christian, but of society as well. Therefore, I believe that the greatest revival is yet to come. And I believe that this revival will be the final opportunity God gives humankind before the rapture. It is for this reason that God is calling His people to prayer and unity. Prayer that is focused on God, instead of on us, will penetrate the darkness and allow the light of God to shine in. This kind of prayer requires spiritual warfare. It requires the spirit of Elijah, which among other things, necessitates boldness to speak truth to power and to release the supernatural power of His love into the lives of others.

I advise you, pray as you have never prayed before, read the Word of God as if it were the last time you would read it, worship as if it were your last opportunity to worship. Focus on your crown, on what God is about to do, and on the celebration that heaven is about to give you. Think with the mind of Christ, for the best is yet to come.

Our boat will not sink! He said, "Let us go to the other side." That means we are going to make it because we have territories to conquer, demons to cast out, and miracles and wonders to perform.

Chapter Eight
UNDER SIEGE

THE CHURCH OF Jesus Christ is under siege. Our enemy, knowing his time is almost over, has launched a strategic attack against us with the sole purpose of breaking us down to the point of surrender. Our families, marriages, ministries, and finances are all under siege.

In 2 Kings 6:24–33, we read the story of Syria besieging Samaria. Now, we need to understand that to besiege a city, as in the case of Samaria, an armed force surrounds and isolates it. This military force does not allow those defending the city to get reinforcements or supplies. Its sole purpose is to cause starvation and deprivation.

During the siege, the invading army continues its attack on the city. The warfare continues; flaming arrows, rocks, and many other things continue to rain down on the people. Again, its purpose is to greatly weaken the city and cause it to surrender. When the city finally surrenders, the invading army comes in, takes the city, and kills most of the people while taking women and children captive.

I repeat, we are under siege, and it is the enemy's intent to put layers of heaviness on us so as to break our morale. He has surrounded us, hindered our prayers, and frustrated us because he wants us to become weary and give up. He wants us to accept what is coming as if it is hopeless to resist.

This kind of warfare makes you feel as if you can't

go on. Heaven seems to be closed, and you go from one attack to another. The truth is that it doesn't get better, and you find yourself going through such difficulties that it stretches your faith to the breaking point. You are fighting spiritual forces and not human forces; therefore, you must not back down and listen to the enemy's lies. You can't simply allow him to intimidate you because you have a calling that you just can't put down.

However, when you feel that you can no longer wait on God, you will come to the conclusion that you must take action—and when you act on your own, you will end up doing things you never imagine you would do.

> Then, as the king of Israel was passing by the wall, a woman cried out to him, saying, "Help, my lord, O king!" And he said, "If the LORD does not help you, where can I find help for you? From the threshing floor or from the winepress?" Then the king said to her, "What is troubling you?" And she answered, "This woman said to me, 'Give your son that we may eat him today, and we will eat my son tomorrow.' So we boiled my son, and ate him. And I to her on the next day, 'Give your son that we may eat him'; but she has hidden her son."
> —2 KINGS 6:26–29

Observe: a woman approached this mother with what seemed to be a solution for survival. This other woman took from her that which is priceless—her son, her future, her destiny—and convinced her to kill her own seed. She convinced her that killing and eating her child was alright. In her desperation, she took action because she did not trust the Lord.

As a pastor for over 27 years, I am amazed at what

people do simply because they don't believe. We take that which was birthed out of us and offer it on the altar of death because someone convinced us that the temporal was more important than the eternal. God planted a seed in us—a vision, a purpose, and a future—and when things get really bad, we sacrifice our destiny for a quick release. We forget that all things work out for good for those who would believe.

Sometimes you have got to live what you preach. Sometimes you have got to touch what you sing. This is more than a "hallelujah" or a "praise the Lord"; this is a life and death matter that requires our absolute obedience to Him that gave His life for us. Not all of us are going to get a free "get out of jail card" like Peter did in Acts 12:5–10. Some of us will die as James did at the hands of Herod. Accept this reality; you no longer live for yourself, and the life which you now live in the flesh you live by faith in the Son of God (Gal. 2:20).

But the problem with dealing with the devil is that he always has something up his sleeve. When it's his turn to give up what he promised you, he reneges and breaks his promise. He told you that if you would go your own way, he would partner with you, and you would survive. But the devil is a deceiver, and you believed him.

When you awaken (the next morning), you are going to find out that not only can he not produce that which he promised you, but also that you have just eaten your future, your seed. Shame always comes the day after. At the beginning, everything makes sense to the one who walks under his own wisdom. It takes a little time, but eventually that decision will blow up, and all will see the foolishness of what we have done.

This woman's lack of spiritual maturity caused her to

go to the king and not the prophet. She appealed to the son of a murderer for help because in her eyes, he was in a position of authority, when in reality he was not. You can't stand on human power; you need to stand on divine authority so that you can have a breakthrough. You can't break this kind of siege; you can't do it on your own or with something or someone that has no divine revelation. Human efforts and strategies are useless because the pressure to respond humanly is so great. You must gain your position of authority—and that can only come through an active surrender and dependence on the Lord.

We spend so much time and effort fighting with each other that we don't even realize what we are doing. We are one body! We need each other, and we need to stop eating ourselves. We spend so much time fighting battles God has never called us to fight that now we don't have the strength to fight the battle we *were* called to fight. We are depressed, weak, and weary. We are walking away from ministry, marriage, and fellowship. We emulate the king—tearing off our robes, stirring our anger, and blaming others for our condition.

I decree and declare that our boat will not sink; we will make it to the other side because we have territories to conquer, demons to cast out, and miracles to perform. I will not pay attention to the storm that is upon me; if Jesus is asleep in the boat, He must have a good reason. Maybe it's because He said, "Let's go to the other side!"

God spoke again through His prophet (2 Kings 7:1, NLT) and stated that by "this time tomorrow" there would be abundance in the city. God made a statement, a declaration that He would put an end to the siege. But who will believe the word of the Lord? The spirit is willing, but the flesh is weak. To stand in a position of trust you must first believe that God will do what He has said He would do. That means you don't put your hand on it. You just trust Him for your health, finances, problems, etc. But how can we do that when our faith is so weak and the attacks on our lives continue unabated? My response is this: we must start by stirring the fire of God that is in us. Our heart holds the fire of God; it must not go out. That means that you and I need to tend to it. Darkness wants to suffocate our fire, but you and I must continue to stir the fire.

Prayer stirs the fire. We have to pray in the morning, at midday, and in the evening. You must stir it when you don't feel like doing it, even if it is just for a few minutes. You must do it anyway, anyhow. Keep in mind that you weren't meant to live outside of the fire; you were meant to live in the glory, in the presence of God. Continued prayer and worship will cause the fire to come alive in you and allow you to resist the siege that has surrounded you. It will also give you the courage to declare that which is not as though it were. Then you will rise up like an eagle and take your place of authority.

The altar of your heart needs a sacrifice on it. You can't have a breakthrough without a sacrifice. God is calling us to lay down our lives and become a living sacrifice. That means you stay the course, and you walk it out, even at the cost of your own life. These things I have learned in my journey of life with Him.

I have also learned that there is always a critic in the crowd. When God speaks, there is always someone who questions the heart of God—and that is extremely dangerous. No sooner had the man of God spoken on behalf of the Father than "an officer on whose hand the king leaned answered the man of God and said, 'Look, if the Lord would make windows in heaven, could this thing be?'"

(2 Kings 7:2). Here is a leader who could not lead because he had lost the Spirit of the Father and had acquired the spirit of another.

He had the spirit of the king, who had certain knowledge and authority but no revelation. Some folks just don't get it. Knowledge without revelation leads to failure. And revelation can only be found in the presence of God, not in books, slogans, or degrees. Where there is no revelation, the people perish because a critical spirit always comes to bring confusion and doubt. This young man received within himself the spirit of his king. My question is, "Who speaks into your life—the king or the prophet?"

The prophet responded to the statement of the young officer: "In fact, you shall see it with your eyes, but you shall not eat of it" (2 Kings 7:2). When we speak in foolishness, the errors of our ways will be revealed, and consequences will soon follow. The power of life and death is in the tongue; therefore, you must be careful as to what comes out of your mouth. When you or I speak against what God has already spoken into existence, we curse ourselves. I believe that if there is something that upsets God the most, it is that He is not believed, especially by those who claim to represent Him. The prophet tells the young man, "Son, you're going to see the blessing; you're going to know that there is abundance. But you will not eat of this harvest because you refused to believe."

Now, there were four men who were lepers at the entrance of the city. They were not allowed in the city; a dying city does not allow these contagious people to come in because they have a disease. I wonder how many people we keep out of our churches because we think they are impure and carry some disease that might kill us. They sat by the gate talking to each other, and they said, "Why are we sitting here waiting to die? If we stay here, we die, and if somehow we get in the city, we will also die. So, let's just go over to the enemy's camp, and if they kill us, well then, we die" (see 2 Kings 7:3-4).That is the mindset of those who realize they have nothing to lose. And that should be our attitude as Christians.

At twilight, they went to the enemy's camp, and when they came to the edge of the camp, no one was there. The Lord had caused the enemy to hear the sound of the armies of heaven approaching. This caused panic in the camp, and they took off running in the middle of the night, leaving everything behind.

Observe this: while the people in the city were eating each other, wasting time complaining, and fighting with each other, God was defeating their enemies, and they didn't even know it. No one was watching the enemy's camp—they were too busy with internal affairs, concerned with hunger, and looking for solutions that produced nothing.

Forgive me for repeating myself, but church, we need to stop the fighting, division, and the killing of each other. As long as we are building our little kingdom, we will never see the big picture. We are commanded to love one another; it's not a choice but a command. If we would cry out to our God with one voice, heaven would hear and send its armies to our defense. The devil and his demons will have no choice but to take off running, because they know what a mighty God we serve. Hell knows who our Jesus is; it's about time that we also know Him in a new dimension—the way Peter, John, and James knew Him when He transformed Himself before their eyes on the mountaintop (Matt. 17:1-2).

The lepers went from one tent to another, eating,

drinking, and carrying away silver and gold. I want to tell you this: you're going to get back everything the devil stole from you with *interest!* Finally the lepers said, "This is not right; today is a day of good news, and we are not sharing it. We've got to go back and tell the people that the siege is over!" (see 2 Kings 7:9). So they went back and told the gatekeepers, who told the king. But nobody would believe them. The four lepers kept trying to tell someone, "The enemy's camp is empty; come and see the glory of God!"

I want to tell you today: this is going to turn around! We may be under a siege, but tomorrow is coming; a new day is coming; a day of abundance is coming. The camp is empty; we just haven't seen it yet. But I tell you, it's empty! So I am not giving up because I can hear the roaring lion. I can hear the armies of the Lord. They are coming; the Lord is coming, so lift up your voice and praise Him.

Finally, they sent out scouts; they found a road full of clothing, equipment, money, and food. The people ran out of the city with so much force that they trampled to death the young officer. He saw, but he could not touch because he would not believe (2 Kings 7:17). Will you believe?

Elijah's biography can be written in two words: Elijah prayed. Prayer is a must; travailing prayer is a must. He who prays can move the hand of God.

Chapter Nine
PRAYER ALTARS

When I was a little boy living in Puerto Rico, our church required that every family have a prayer altar gathering every Monday in their homes. In fact, it was a custom in our Latin countries to practice the coming together as a family to worship, read the Word, and pray.

We always had one evening a week for a prayer service in our churches, another day (Monday) to pray in our homes, and of course, everyone had what we called a prayer closet in their homes where they would pray every day. Also, somewhere in our homes, usually in the living room or in a bedroom, we would have a place where we would put an open Bible, a hymnbook, and some literature. We would use these when we gathered together for prayer. We all understood the importance and power of prayer.

While we had a place to pray and worship our God in our homes and churches, there were many people in our communities who practiced witchcraft and had their own prayer altars. On those altars, they would place pictures, candles, and a number of things that satanic priests would use to get in contact with their spiritual masters and to exert evil influence over the region.

I will never forget my experience in the little Assemblies of God church in Ponce, Puerto Rico. Our pastor had just rented the first floor of a building for our new sanctuary. Little did he know that the second floor of that same building had a spiritual center in it where a satanic priest would hold gatherings and do enchantments.

So there we were—a church bearing the light of glory on the first floor and a spiritual center spewing out darkness on the second. When the satanic priest realized a Pentecostal church was on the first floor, he started sending evil spirits to drive us away. We, in turn, realized what was happening and started sending Holy Ghost fire up to the second floor.

We had a battle going on; he prayed to his god, and we prayed to our God. I don't need to tell you who lost. I believe he suffered a heart attack and was taken out in a stretcher. Our prayers started a revival that caused such an uproar in that community that hundreds came to the feet of Jesus. This was an area in Ponce where the police dared not enter unless they were fully armed and came in caravans. Something happened when a small group of men and women built a prayer altar in that community; it brought transformational revival to an entire region!

Let me be clear and explain to you that a prayer altar is simply a place where you meet with God. It can be at home, in a church, at work, or even in your car. It is simply a place where you and God meet. I am not talking about idol worship or the burning of candles, etc., so commonly known to those of us who come from the Caribbean and Central and South America; please do not get confused. In the simplest of terms, it is a place where you and God meet.

However, we need to go deeper than just having prayer time and a location. A prayer altar has to be much more than praying a daily prayer. For a prayer altar to be effective, it must be a place where you travail until you break through the forces of darkness that hinder your prayer, enter into the presence of God, and see His purposes manifested over the prevailing spiritual climate in your region.

In other words, it must be more than your morning devotion. It calls for a set-apart life, a holy priesthood, and living in covenant. The foremost altar is your heart (Matt. 5:23–24; Luke 6:45; Col. 3:1); true prayer and worship should begin there. You and I have become a temple of the Holy Spirit, and in us He dwells. Let us first turn inward to find that place where the fire of God flows.

What if every believer established a personal and family prayer altar that would draw the presence and purposes of God into their lives and homes?

What if every pastor and church would establish a prayer altar that drew the presence and power of God that would push back the forces of darkness in their communities and manifest the purposes of God?

What if pastors and churches would come together to raise the level of prayer above the level of darkness that prevails over the minds and lifestyles of people living in the land? I believe we would see true transformation taking place.

What if every school, hospital, business, and government agency had a prayer altar where darkness was renounced and the presence and blessings of God were sought? Imagine raising the level of prayer so high that the workers of darkness were helpless to hold back a tsunami of transforming revival and righteousness.

To draw the presence and purposes of God we must begin with our own act of devotion—an offering of ourselves as a living sacrifice, a life of communion with the

God who called us out of captivity and set us as priests in His kingdom.

Elijah built an altar to the Lord, and the people experienced a visible manifestation of God's power (1 Kings 18:36–39). A manifestation of God's reality and presence was needed in the land of Israel. Today we find ourselves in a desperate need for God's presence.

Throughout the Bible, when God's people found themselves in these circumstances, they were led to raise up prayer altars and call on the name of the Lord. If we, as a priesthood of believers, will raise up prayer altars where God has placed us, we too can see the purposes and power of God manifested.

We must create an atmosphere for Him to come and abide with us so that the real work of restoration and redemption can begin in our land. I don't know when Jesus is coming back; I don't have a time or a place. What I do know is that when He comes back, I better be doing what He told me to do. Too many of us are just sitting back, waiting on the rapture, and disconnecting ourselves from the reality that surrounds us. But we must be about the Father's business. A nation was once in spiritual darkness, and they needed a prophet to build an altar. What about today?

> God is seeking for righteous men and women to go beyond a five-minute prayer and a three-verse Bible study. He is seeking for us to raise up prayer altars so we may set in place a net of effective fervent prayer all over the land, in every nation, all across the globe.[1]

I have noticed that whenever we abandon (1 Kings 18:30) the prayer altar, whenever we stop travailing and just go through the motions, darkness and wickedness increase, and the consequences are bondage and death. However, whenever there has been desperation for deliverance and returning to the Lord, the first order of business was to restore the altar (2 Chron. 15:8).

We have got to go beyond just praying for our own well-being or blessings. Join something that is bigger than your world. Pray for the nations and their leaders; pray for revival, transformation, and awakening. Pray to create an atmosphere into which God is being drawn and manifested. We usually pray for our ministries, church, and health, etc. But this is bigger than me and my little kingdom; no ministry, church, or denomination, no matter how big, could ever single-handedly do the work of bringing His kingdom into any nation. We must come together and build a net of prayer all over this land.

Pastor John Mulinde observes that we don't realize that the darkness in the land is affecting us. The things we see on television, what is allowed at school, and even the mindset of the people is also affecting the church. A church in a land where darkness is flooding in is being affected by that darkness. It is being drawn into a place of slumber, blindness, and powerlessness. The church sees the ungodly things that are going on, but has no faith or power to see them changed.

We seek to build these prayer altars in our hearts, homes, churches, marketplaces, and all over the world so that we can push back and pierce the darkness over our land. When we do that, His light, glory, and fire will descend upon the people, opening their eyes, and giving them a final opportunity to turn to Him and be saved.

Remember that we have been given legal authority by God to control the direction of our society. Spiritual forces were not given dominion over the Earth; man was (Gen. 1:28). But when man chooses to yield his authority to spiritual forces, darkness comes in, suffocates spiritual life, and hardens hearts. The heavens are closed up and evil prevails. When this happens, we lose the ability to hear God clearly, for we have no deep communion with the Lord. We become religious with no ability or power to execute God's will. Therefore, we need to awaken and run into His presence so that we are able to receive instruction and revelation for such a time as this.

God created us so that we may rule over the Earth, not the devil. For any spiritual power to exercise authority in the land, we must be involved. This means that no demons or angels can rule anything or anywhere on Earth without our authority. This is why priesthood is so important. The priest has the authority to influence the spiritual realm as well as the physical world. He holds the key to open and close doors. Are we not a royal priesthood, a chosen generation? (1 Pet. 2:9–10). Listen, we have been given authority to rule; it's time to use it!

Priesthood is not just saying prayers to God. Priesthood has an element of being set apart from the world, coming to the Word of God, submitting to God, and yielding ourselves to His will. Once we return to the place we have been called to and restore the prayer altar, we will see a harvest of souls come into the kingdom of God. I am ready for a harvest.[2]

Endnotes

1. John Mulinde and Mark Daniel, *Prayer Altars: A Strategy that Is Changing Nations* (Orlando, FL: World Trumpet Mission, 2013), 10.

2. Note: Special thanks to Pastors Don Campbell, Ben Abell, Mark Daniel, and John Mulinde for their notes on this topic. For

more information about prayer altars and how you can receive training in this area, please contact World Trumpet Missions at media@worldtrumpet.com and purchase your copy of *Prayer Altars*.

We must go beyond our own ministry, church, fellowship, or denomination. If ever the church of Jesus Christ needed to come together, rise up, and step into her destiny, it is now.

Chapter Ten

THE BUILDING OF A MULTICULTURAL PRAYER ARMY

Nehemiah received a report of the terrible conditions of those who stayed behind in Jerusalem. After hearing the report, he sat down, wept, prayed, and fasted for many days. During this process, he received a vision from the Lord: to rebuild the walls of Jerusalem.

Seeing the condition and having a vision is not enough; we need to have a godly plan. Nehemiah, with God's help and direction, formulated a plan, and when he went before the king, he was able to answer the king's questions in reference to his journey.

I believe that we are not only called to pray but also to act. Prayer is not enough; it must go hand in hand with action. We can cry out to God, but if we don't serve the needy, the elderly, the widow, and the poor, we are only doing a segment of what God requires. I also believe that we need to speak truth (in love) to power—political and religious power. There is an anointing that some men and women of God have that allows them to rise up and speak into the hearts of other leaders, causing them to align themselves with God's will.

Not everyone can do this, certainly not an immature prophet who doesn't know when to be quiet and when to speak. These are seasoned men and women of God that the Lord has prepared for such a time as this; these we need to hear. The bottom line is that without an action plan, we will end up going around in circles, wasting both our time and God's.

Though there are many prayer movements going on around the world, not every one of them functions or operates in the same way. There are different strategies in different regions of the world, and only through prayer can we know exactly which strategies God wants us to implement in our region. What works in the Philippines may or may not work here; therefore, we need to find the heart of God so that the Holy Spirit can bring rain on our fields.

Life and ministry become frustrating and disappointing when we don't know where we are going. First, we need to understand that we are part of a larger puzzle. God's plans are for the nations; therefore, He puts a group of diverse people together so that corporately they can change the course of a nation. This means that we need to know the God-given purpose of the nation we live in because God has a plan for each and every nation of the world. When you wrap yourself in your own community, revolve everything around your own local church, and build walls around your own ministry, you limit God. He said, "Ask Me for the nations…"

Second, we need to understand that our priority is to make sure we are in the place we need to be when He calls. John the Baptist was born to prepare the way of the Lord. He wasn't bird watching when the Lord needed him. David was born to lead a nation; he wasn't playing cards with his friends when the Lord needed him. Both of them, and many others that the Lord called, were clear in their identity and knew their destiny.

He who doesn't know who he is and doesn't have a plan from God to take him to where he needs to go will run after any offer. That is our problem; we are out of place. Some of us do not need to be pastors, but rather teachers, evangelists, or psalmists. But we were taught that we all needed to pastor. No, we need to be in the place He assigned us so that when that moment comes, we can rise up in our gifting and anointing and bring transformation to a hurting world. I believe that he who truly knows God and His purpose for his life will not allow relationships, problems, offers, or money to stand in the way of his God-given destiny.

Third, lay hands over your disciples. Those who have been assigned to you must have your spirit and understand the vision. Transfer your anointing, your wisdom, grace, and power to your spiritual children. Do as Moses and Jesus did; it will help you in your journey.

Fourth, evaluate. Let's be real: Some folk are going to leave you; others are going to get tired along the way; and there will be conflicts. Don't get discouraged because someone betrayed you. Welcome to the club of those who have been betrayed by those we have imparted and invested in, only to have them rise up against us and try to kill our influence. Those who ate with us have now become our enemies. This is a part of the ministry that none of us like, yet it is still part of the ministry. A son's betrayal is not going to stop me from giving and imparting.

Fifth, get a letter. Find out what documents you need that will allow you to reveal who you are to others and be accepted. A passport reveals who I am and allows me to enter a country. A visa allows me to reveal who I am—and the stamp on it reveals not only my identity, but also indicates that I am accepted in that territory. Joseph stood before his brothers and revealed who he was and was accepted by them as one who had been placed in authority over them. Your anointing is your letter; it will break the yoke of indifference as others will see who you truly are and accept you. Stop trying to impress and manipulate your way; God's hand will lead you to the right door. People are doors, and they will help you to get to where you need to go. Learn not to reject the door God has opened for you. If the Red Sea opens up, go through. The wind is blowing, and your anointing will make a way for you. Remember, get your letter.

All of this requires an anointing to love Him to the degree that our hearts burn for His purposes. Generally, we ask for anointing to preach or teach, etc. But the greater anointing is to stay in His love. That love anointing will not only allow us to believe and obey Him, but it will also allow us to not hold anything back from Him. We yield to Him.

Our top priority is therefore to love Him. Before we go to the capital and march around, before we set strategies and plans into place, we need to do what is first. And what is first is to love Him. Prayer, fasting, and reading the Word is not a discipline; it is how we have communion with Him. These we need to do.

Our identity is not our assignment. Everything we do will cause us to get tired and weary, but His love will carry us through; it will compel us to move forward. Therefore, the core of our identity is to love Him. I believe the Spirit is trying to stir the church back to this love for Him—for it will take a loving church to change the course of this nation.

How can we awaken a sleeping church? Must tragedy come once again to our doorstep? Will an economic tsunami turn us back to God? I have no answers for these questions. Yet I do know that we need a prayer army to rise up that will provoke a move of God of the likes of Pentecost. We need the church to pray—not just a group in the church—but the corporate church.

I constantly have people tell me about their prayer movement. But most of the time we pray within our own groups. Blacks, Whites, Asians, and Hispanics all have a prayer movement, yet we refuse to pray together. We use language, cultures, and styles of prayer as excuses. We need to stop this; our nation is going to hell in a handbasket, and all we do is argue about foolishness.

Darkness is increasing, and we need God's people to come together to push back the darkness over the land so that those who are in bondage can see the light of His glory and be saved. The night is coming when no one can work; our time is running out. Church, wake up, for death is at your doorstep, and you are sound asleep.

I believe that the only way we can position our region for revival is through prayer, consecration, and unity. We must create an atmosphere that will draw the presence of God, push back the forces of darkness, and allow the Holy Spirit to bring forth a greater manifestation of the kingdom of God. Travailing prayer, extravagant worship, acts of kindness, and unity will allow us to do that.

A nation's destiny is distributed among its people; no one has a monopoly on it. When you reject someone who is different from you, you lose out on their gifting. Your denomination, fellowship, or faith camp doesn't have all it takes to bring about God's destiny for our nation. We need each other in order to prepare and raise up a multicultural prayer army (movement) that will bring true transformation to our nation.

We need to get back to being what we were called to be—children of light, shining bright for all to see. Let it shine, let it shine, let it shine!

Chapter Eleven
THIS LITTLE LIGHT OF MINE

Jesus said to His disciples; "I have come as a light into the world, that whoever believes in Me should not abide in darkness" (John 12:46). Later He added, "I am going away, but I will send you a helper, the Holy Spirit. He will not only be by you, but in you" (John 14:26; 15:26; 16:7). This means that through Christ we have become children of light; the light of glory is in us!

We must never forget that we are a chosen generation, a royal priesthood, a holy nation. He called us out of darkness into His marvelous light, and now God is in us, and we are complete (1 Pet. 2:9–11). For He said; "I am the light of the world. He who follows Me shall not walk in darkness, but have the light of life" (John 8:12).

He has made us light. We carry the light, and He has called us to live in that light. But the darkness that surrounds us wants to suffocate our light. We are pursued, persecuted, and rejected—not only by demons, but by religious people who love darkness more than light, who love this world and the things of it. They do this, even though the Word of God says, "Don't love the world nor the things it offers you, for when you love the world, you do not have the love of the Father in you" (1 John 2:15, NLT).

I have found that the greatest persecution and harm that can be done to the body of Christ comes from individuals who profess that they are Christians, yet the fruit of the Spirit cannot be found in them. They are as one who is torn between two lovers; it's hard to be faithful when you are being pulled in two different directions. Sooner or later your light starts to dim, and eventually it goes out because you have another lover.

You might say to me, "Bishop, you can't judge me. You don't really know me or how I live my life." My response is, "Yes, I can see that your light is not shining as it shone before. You can go to church, shout, and praise the Lord. You can quote Scripture, sing, and tell everyone how grateful you are. All that is fine, but it doesn't take away from the fact that your light is not shining as it did before."

When we do things that bring shame to the name of Jesus, when we dishonor His holy name by our behavior and actions, when we abuse our freedom and justify what we do under the banner of grace, our light isn't shining too bright. I hear Christians testify about how greatly God has blessed them, while having an affair with their brother's wife. Your own words condemn you.

Listen, when you handle the Word of God deceitfully so you can do what you want to do, you put a veil over the gospel, and you partner with the god of this age. Don't be angry with me; I need you to understand that your actions blind the minds of the people so that they don't believe and the light of God does not get through (2 Cor. 4:2–4).

When you don't stir the flame that is inside of you with prayer, worship, and the study of the Word, your light diminishes. These spiritual exercises are what keep you on the path and birth the life and mind of God in your heart. Never forget that you are the light of the world set upon a hill. You cannot hide, for you have been placed on a lamp stand so you can give light to all those around you. Remember, everything you do reflects Him. He has made us a light...and we are called to shine like bright lights.

We shine so that a people who sit in darkness can see the great light that is coming from us. Those who sit in the regions and shadows of death must know that the light of God has dawned. That broken man, that hurting woman, that crying child must see the light so that hope can arise in them. This little light of mine must shine, shine, shine in this vast darkness—and when that happens, darkness cannot and will not overtake it!

Those who are grateful for what He has done for them will do whatever it takes because they are thankful. Their acts of kindness are birthed out of a heart that is full of love. Ministry is not a burden, but a joy, and they understand that through their light, people can find Jesus, the Savior of humankind.

Sadly, most of us spend our days looking for what we want, and we are always aware of what we don't have. We need to redirect our focus and see what we have been given. Can we count the miracles He has done? Can we remember the times He has provided, delivered, protected, and strengthened us? Oh, we humans are so short in memory, so quick to complain.

We need to get back to being what we were called to be—children of light, shining bright for all to see. Let's sing again that old song we used to sing: "This little light of mine, I'm going to let it shine...let it shine, let it shine, let it shine."

Our nation which proclaims "In God We Trust" has rejected her God, and her rejection has caused us to lose His protection. In my view, America is now a nation in captivity. In 2015, there were 355 incidents of mass killings where four or more people were killed. We are all awaiting the next terrorist attack, and to be frank, many people live behind locked doors in fear for their lives as the violence keeps spreading and spreading. We, the church, are guilty for the darkness over the land, for we have not done our job. If we had been the voice of God to a lost generation, if we had taken a stand and not been silent, if we had stopped building our own kingdoms, instead of the kingdom of God, America would not be covered in darkness today.

But we have allowed ourselves to be intimidated. They set into action their humanist agenda, took over our children's education, put activist judges in place, and changed laws (among other things), while we were behind closed doors having church. Whenever someone would bring to our attention the conditions that surrounded us, we declared that Jesus was coming back and we were leaving in the rapture. We basically said, "To hell with them."

Somewhere in the journey we forgot what Jesus said in John 9:4–5: "I must work the works of Him who sent Me while it is day; the night is coming when no one can work. As long as I am in the world, I am the light of the world." Well, now they are coming into our churches and telling us what we can and cannot do. They want to turn off our lights and let darkness reign. We must emulate Jesus and declare as He did that as long as we are in the world, we will be the light of the world.

God was not caught off guard with the spiritual fall of America. He has kept a remnant of prayer warriors who worship in spirit and truth all across this nation. They are a people, set by God in a region, who understand that there is a time to weep and a time to fight. Well, my brothers and sisters, I believe the time to fight has arrived! For God says, "So take a new grip with your tired hands and strengthen your weak knees. Mark out a straight path for your feet so that those who are weak and lame will not fall but become strong" (Heb. 12:12–13, NLT).

There comes a time when all weeping must end, when you must shake the dust off, rise above your grieving, and get back in the fight. I grew up in the streets of New York City, and I learned a very important lesson when I was very young: when you are under attack, you have got to fight back. We are under attack, and we must fight back; we must fight for our faith. Greater is He who is inside of us than he who is in the world.

There may be many churches closing in America, but mine isn't one of them! There may be many pastors resigning in America, but I'm not quitting! There may be many churches and ministers that have lost their voice in the community, but we are not one of them. We will speak truth, anointed truth, to power, and out of us the unlimited power of God will be released, birthing a transformational revival that will cover the land—and then we can go home.

God birthed or brought us here; He placed us here, set us upon the hill, and it's about time we stop complaining about why we are here and start doing what we were brought here to do in the first place—which is shine and fight!

My city of Baltimore, the city that I love, has a terrible reputation across the country. Our murder rate, heroin epidemic, AIDS, and the Freddie Gray riots have caused people to ask me, "Can anything good come out of Baltimore?" My response is yes, yes, yes!

God is giving us the city—a place whose name means circle of Baal, a place where people sit in darkness, a region where the shadow of death reigns—and He has declared that we would see a great light, the light of God over our city. The devil knows what is going on and has sent all his forces against us to destroy our city. We know why he is doing this; he wants to cause us to step back, be intimidated, and stop shining. But we will not stop; we are sanctifying ourselves because tomorrow God will do wonders among us (Josh. 3:5).

God is making Baltimore a city of refuge. He is not going to get rid of the guilty and clean up the city. No, He is going to transform the city so that it is a place where the rejected, hurting, and guilty can run to—because in our city there is light. How can I state this so boldly? I can state this, because this little light of mine is already shining—and not by itself; thousands of us are gathering in prayer and action. It's a multicultural army that cannot be stopped.

Why am I so sure of this? Because God has given us prophetic insight—the ability to hear and see what others cannot see. Five years ago, the Lord told us to blow the trumpet in the city and call His people to prayer. He said, "For My people will hear the sound of the trumpet and will come."

Then a pastor from Africa by the name of John Mulinde came to the city and told some of us and reminded others that we were the East Gate of America. He told us that revival will come through this gate and sweep the nation. He also told us that many people from around the world have been praying for our city.

Throughout the years, many men and women of God have come to this city and region declaring the will of God for all to hear. There have been so many pastors and bishops that have given their all for this cause. These eagles have flown through the storms; in the middle of the turmoil, they fly with the breath of God, and now, I believe, we shall see and touch that which they dreamed.

Yet, I am not naïve to the evil that surrounds us. I understand spiritual warfare and the strategies of Satan's disciples who seek to turn our nation into a humanistic one—separated from God and persecuting those of us who still believe in divine order.

Let us remember these words of Albert Einstein who left Germany in the midst of the turbulence accompanying the Nazi rise to power:

> Being a lover of freedom, when the [Nazi] revolution came, I looked to the universities to defend it, knowing that they had always boasted of their devotion to the cause of truth; but no, the universities took refuge in *silence*. Then I looked to the great editors of the newspapers, whose flaming editorials in days gone by had proclaimed their love of freedom; but they, like the universities, were *silenced* in a few short weeks. I then addressed myself to the authors, to those who had passed themselves off as the intellectual guides of Germany, and among whom was frequently discussed the question of freedom and its place in modern life. They are in turn, very dumb. Only the *church* stood squarely across the path of Hitler's campaign for suppressing the truth. I never had any special interest in the church before, but now I feel a great affection and admiration for it because the church alone has had the courage and persistence to stand for intellectual truth and moral freedom. I am forced to confess that what I once despised I now praise unreservedly.[1]

Today, we must also stand for truth and be a light unto the nations. We will not be intimidated, we will not back down, and we will not run. Let the world know that there is an army, a multicultural army that comes onto the battlefield in the name that is above all other names, the name of Jesus!

ENDNOTE

1. Albert Einstein, *Time* magazine, vol 36, no. 26 (23 December 1940), emphasis mine.

When God promises you something, it is because He has already prepared it for you. He announces to you what is about to happen before it happens— because for Him, it has already happened.

Chapter Twelve
PREPARING FOR WHAT HAS BEEN PREPARED FOR US

THE FUNNY THING about us human beings is that when God gives us a word, we get all excited about it—and in the end, we do absolutely nothing with that which we have received from Him. We simply do not pursue it.

If we allow our daily struggles, agendas, challenges that life brings, or even our feelings to direct our actions, that word becomes just a wasted word. The Word of God says that Saul was called to reign, but when the time came to sit in the chair that had been prepared for him, he disappeared and was found hiding among the equipment.

God has already told us (Ps. 23:5) that He has prepared a table for us in the presence of our enemies. In spite of our problems and difficulties, we must press on, for we are called to raise the level of prayer in our region, serve our community in love, and pierce the darkness with the arrow of worship so that the light of His glory can be revealed.

This can only be done when we understand the power that exists in unity. When one person prays, a thousand will flee, but when two pray, they put ten thousand to flight (Deut. 32:30). This is the power of unity; efforts are multiplied. Now, imagine what would happen if the entire church prayed. I believe we would see things we have never seen since the days of Christ. Didn't He say we would do greater works than He did?

Pentecost came through the power of prayer; the heavens were opened through the power of prayer; miracles happened through the power of prayer. One man was in prison, yet his chains fell off his hands through the power of prayer. Two men were in prison, yet the ground shook and the gates of the prison swung open through the power of prayer. Three men prayed in a furnace, yet the fire could not kill them through the power of prayer! Church, we need to pray and pray and pray; we need to pray until something happens.

Revival is carried in prayer, transformation is carried in prayer, and what we have been called to do can only be done through the power of prayer. Prayer changes us, and those who are called to change the world must first be changed themselves.

He who does not pray cannot sustain on his shoulders the anointing he carries; eventually, he will succumb to the weight and resign himself to accepting God's permissible will instead of His perfect will. For many of us, just getting in the room (permissible will) is enough. Yet, for those who understand that they have been called to the head of the table (perfect will), nothing less than that is acceptable.

The perfect will of God will not allow that which has been reserved for you to be held back. There comes a time when that which has been promised to you must come to pass (1 Sam. 9:23–24). You must, however, be in place—seated and aligned with His perfect will. Prayer aligns and sustains your faith to believe that which is impossible. It opens your heart to accept His grace and launches you into your destiny.

When God promises you something, it is because He has already prepared it; He has laid it aside for you (Eccles. 3:15). He doesn't say something and then make it happen sometime later. Samuel told the cook, "Bring the portion which I gave you, of which I said to you, 'Set it apart.'" Then he said to Saul, "Here it is, what was kept back. It was set apart for you" (1 Sam. 9:23–24). What God has promised you has already been prepared; it has your name on it. You must claim it, confess it, and decree it in the name of Jesus. Take hold of that which has been given to you.

Understand this: He announces to you and me what is about to happen before it happens—because for Him, it has already happened (Isa. 42:9). God starts from the end to the beginning; we start from the beginning to the end; and when we meet, fulfillment happens. We walk by faith toward the promised word. This requires two key elements: obedience and discipline.

Again, I say that Saul could never sit in the chair that was prepared for him because he had no discipline to obey. His insecurities got in the way because he could never see himself as God saw him. All these things happened because he didn't prepare his heart for what had been prepared for him; he simply didn't prepare for it.

Our prayers should be, "Lord, prepare me to be a vessel that can shine for your glory. Give me the courage and the strength to step into that which you have prepared for me." We must now understand two important things: First, God has prepared a table before us, and second, He has prepared a chair for us to sit on. A table is for eating, to be nourished and strengthened. A chair is to govern, decree, and command. Both are necessary in this present hour.

If you are not prepared to take your seat at the table, someone else will come and take your place. We spend too much time going around in circles, playing musical chairs, concerned about the affairs of this life instead of taking our seat. Our excuse is that we always have something to do before we can take our place and sit down. Simply put, we are hearers but not doers of His Word.

Now, to sit in the chair of authority, you need to understand the power of His Word. You cannot order angels or demons unless you have faith; faith comes from hearing, the hearing of the Word. Therefore, if I have the Word of God in me, I have faith. And if I have faith, I also have power.

This power allows me to declare that which is not as though it was. I can therefore speak life to that which is dead; I can speak truth to elicit power and produce miracles and wonders as I release that which is inside of me into the spirit of another. The king, president, governor, mayor, etc., will hear what I speak under the anointing of the Holy Spirit and not only receive it, but act upon it in Jesus's name.

Keep in mind that I am not saying anything that is birthed in me, but rather what I hear the Spirit say to me while I am at my prayer altar. God speaks to me; I repeat what He said to me and release it into the atmosphere. When God hears me repeat what He has already said, we enter into agreement and the miracle happens.

We need to say what God is saying and not what we want to say. Our prophetic word does not come to pass—because He didn't say it, we did. We are therefore pushed aside and called names because when we went to speak to the king, we were intimidated or prideful and said what we thought made sense. Here is where brokenness is so important—because when I am broken, dead, and no longer live, I am not afraid of what may happen. I have no agenda; I am not looking for a position or to launch my agenda. The only agenda I have is the agenda of the Lamb of God.

I understand that no trial, persecution, or violence that comes against me shall prosper. God's plans and purposes shall be fulfilled, and all the devils in hell can't stop it. Knowing this truth, I remove myself from my place of comfort and walk about in my Father's business in peace. I believe God, and because I believe Him, I move and do. This reality has not escaped me: the just shall live by faith, plain and simple.

Faith is activated when we say what God says. When we confess what God has decreed, it will happen. Miracles begin with your mouth. That is why Peter said, "Silver and gold I do not have, but what I do have I give you" (Acts 3:6). That's why Paul and Silas sang in prison; that's why the devil wants to silence us—because he understands the power of the spoken word.

When we approach God and God approaches us, miracles happen. This is what all creation is waiting for: the manifestation of the sons of God. Let all of God's children take their place and do what they were born to do. When this happens, true revival will take place, and those who live in darkness shall see the light. It may just be their last chance to turn to Christ.

As Christians, we need to prepare ourselves for such an assignment. Truth be told, preparation requires a set-apart life, a willingness to shine as children of light, and a passion to say what He says as you take your place in the kingdom of God. In closing, let me reaffirm that this multicultural, multiethnic force is committed to prayer and extravagant worship. It operates under the Spirit of love and seeks to release the oil of unity that would bring the body of Christ together to speak truth to power (both political and religious) with signs and wonders.

In addition to this, the prayer army (movement) will be known for its acts of kindness as it seeks to serve a hurting, broken nation. Therefore, the prayer army's covenant consists of four basic tenets:

- First, travailing prayer and extravagant worship.
- Second, releasing the oil of unity in love.
- Third, signs and wonders.
- Fourth, acts of kindness.

This movement is presently led by a neutral body of leaders from different ministries within the Mid-Atlantic region of the USA. Its meetings consist of praying together, equipping the body of believers, and coming together for special events where we model unity and build relationships in addition to seeking His face.

We know that America is being destroyed from within, that our influence on today's culture has declined drastically, and that the church is divided while our enemy is organized and united. We must therefore rise up and be what we were birthed to be—the salt and light of the world.

ABOUT THE AUTHOR

Bishop Ángel L. Núñez was born in New York City. His father abandoned the home before his birth, and at the tender age of eight, he lost his mother to cancer. This left him in the care of the government institutions and forced him to live from home to home. But God's hand was always upon him, and through divine intervention, he was placed with a Christian family for a few years. It was in this home where a lasting imprint of God's love was deposited into his life. Even after growing up and succumbing to a life of violence and drugs, God's seed of love bore salvation and healing to his broken heart.

Bishop Núñez is married to Deborah, and they have five beautiful children and four grandchildren.

The bishop has been in ministry for over 36 years and is the presiding bishop of the Bilingual Christian Fellowship. He holds a doctorate degree in Divinity with a Masters in Theology. As senior pastor of the Bilingual Christian Church of Baltimore for over 27 years, he still travels as an international evangelist winning souls for Christ. He has traveled to 32 countries carrying a prophetic mantle and a challenging word to the church to rise up and fulfill her destiny in Christ. Bishop Núñez provides an apostolic oversight to ministries, both domestic and abroad—giving instruction, direction, and training to pastors and leaders, equipping them to effectually serve the body of Christ.

In this season of his life, he is sensing a pull to speak out about social injustices and also to bring the church into unity cross-culturally by breaking down the ethnicity barriers. He is the president of the Multicultural Prayer Movement in the Mid-Atlantic region which consists of over 400 churches that are African American, Anglo, Hispanic, African, and Asian. Together, they model the spirit of unity as described in John 17.

Finally, Bishop Núñez has written four books: *Let Me Live Again*, *The Latin Indian Speaks*, *How to Reach Your Destiny*, and *My Father's Mantle*.

CONTACT THE AUTHOR

For more information,
please contact the author at:

Website:
www.bilingualchristianchurch.com
www.mc-pm.net

Email:
www.spanishch@aol.com
Michele@bilingualchristianchurch.com

Facebook: Bishop Ángel Núñez
and Ángel Núñez Ministries

Address:
Ángel Núñez Ministries
6000 Erdman Ave.
Baltimore, MD 21205

For speaking invitations,
please contact us at: 410-483-0100.